Step into the heart of Edith Galvez's home— her kitchen, where simplicity meets flavor. For the first time, Edith shares her most cherished recipes in her debut cookbook, *In Edith's Kitchen.* Perfect for families on the go, this cookbook features quick and satisfying weeknight staples like Chicken with Alfredo Pasta. You'll also find lazy weekend dinners such as Mississippi Pot Roast, comforting classics including Huevos Rancheros and Enchiladas Rojas, and of course decadent desserts like Lemon Blueberry Loaf Cake and Mexican Tiramisu. Packed with a variety of nourishing recipes and sprinkled with the love and care that made Edith a social media favorite, this cookbook is your invitation to flavorful, heartfelt cooking without intimidation.

Growing up, Edith spent summers on her family's ranch in Mexico, savoring the vibrant street foods sold by *esquites* and *paletas* vendors and learning treasured recipes and techniques from her abuela and mother. As she built her own family, she had to balance their busy lives while still enjoying delicious meals.

What began as a personal outlet for her shyness and anxiety became a career when Edith's ASMR-style cooking videos skyrocketed her to fame. Her quiet approach resonated with the Latino community, breaking language barriers and inviting fans into her world. Viral hits like her pasta carbonara and chiles rellenos quickly established her as a go-to source for Mexican-American cooking, beloved by new and seasoned cooks alike. *In Edith's Kitchen* has delicious dishes for every meal of the day and is a perfect addition to any home cook's collection.

In **EDITH'S KITCHEN**

In EDITH'S KITCHEN

Recipes from **My Mostly Mexican-American Home to Yours**

Edith Galvez

with Lauren Deen

Photography by Ashleigh Amoroso

Simon Element
New York   Amsterdam/Antwerp
London   Toronto   Sydney/Melbourne   New Delhi

SIMON
ELEMENT

I dedicate this book to Izzy; without her, there would never have been a book! And to my husband, Brandon, for being my biggest supporter.

CONTENTS

INTRODUCTION

I began creating my TikTok cooking videos mostly for myself. Just highlighting my love of my Mexican food. I never included recipes or measurements or anything. I thought I was just cooking for my husband and daughter, Izzy, and then when an entire community came and joined me, it was a blessing, pure and simple. I'm so happy to share these recipes for the first time in this cookbook designed to teach and inspire people of my generation to cook without intimidation and nourish themselves and their families the way my family has nourished me.

The times we spent on my grandparents' ranch in Mexico are some of my most cherished memories. I loved running through the fields; playing with the chickens, goats, and sheep; getting to ride horses whenever I wanted to; and taking occasional trips to the historic silver-mining town of Guanajuato, where my mom is from and where my abuelo had his little market.

The land, the light, the sounds, smells, and traditions would wash over me on those trips, and they have really informed the person I've become. A lot of that time was spent watching my abuela perform her magic in the kitchen. During those moments, she was stirring pots of beans, charring tomatillos for her salsa verde, mixing, kneading, and pressing the masa dough for her tortillas, which she'd cook on a blazing-hot comal (always flipping the disc with her bare hands!). She never measured a thing, of course! Each delicious dish was pulled together by sight, weight, and feel. Things were ready when they looked and smelled done. No measuring spoons, only heart. Cooking by heart.

On those times we took a trip off the ranch, my very favorite thing was to sample what the street food vendors were selling in the plaza. It was the most exciting thing to walk with my brothers back and forth, struggling to decide what to try. I loved the empanada vendor with all the varieties sold from embroidered napkin–lined baskets. There were vendors selling *esquites* (charred corn salad; page 159), *paletas* (fruit ice pops; page 211), and *diablitos* (spicy fruit snow cones; page 208). This food of my culture made its way deep into my soul on those summertime trips to Mexico.

But the urge to replicate those memories on a plate just wasn't in me, for some reason. My mom had it, and she's an excellent cook; she fed us all her perfect versions of Abuela's classic recipes. Again, there was very little measuring—just more cooking by heart.

Happily, I married an amazing man named Brandon and realized my dream of starting my own family, but life was surprisingly difficult. After giving birth to our daughter, Izzy, I struggled with postpartum depression, which led to eating issues and anxiety. I lost a lot of weight. It was challenging, and I had trouble connecting to my family. To battle my problems, I started to cook a bit, which helped calm me down. As I learned not to be scared of food, I started to make it my goal to emulate my mom and, by her example, my grandmothers. I worked at exploring my roots, the things that could keep me centered and happy, through the authentic Mexican family recipes from the women before me.

Brandon introduced me to ASMR videos, and I found them to be a big help. They were so very calming to watch, and I thought they'd be a great way to deal with my natural shyness. No talking, no stress. Just set up the camera, invite viewers into my space, and show them what I love. One of my first videos was of my Tostadas de Tinga recipe (page 116), and I put it online with no expectations. It went viral, with 10.5 million views! I was so excited, because by this point, cooking had become my safe space, and to get this reaction was unbelievable. When my social media started picking up steam, I said, "I'm going to stick with this and see where it takes me." I'm as surprised as you are with my success! I feel grateful that this is my job!

I also love the fact that my ASMR videos can make a positive impact on the Latino community in this country. They help people who struggle with English by skipping written lists of ingredients, since many are visual learners and can figure out my recipes just by watching what I do and how I do it. But they are also great for seasoned cooks who want a little insight into the foods of Mexico.

I'm grateful for my abuelas and my Mexican heritage, my family, and my husband, but there's truly one person whom I have to thank for inspiring me to take this journey: my little girl, Izzy. Without her, I don't know if I would have found this thing I love so much. Why Izzy? Because she's a very strong-willed and persuasive girl,

and when she was two or three, she basically forced me into the kitchen so she could play at being a chef, cutting things with her little plastic knives. To keep her company, I started going back to my memories and cooking the dishes of my family, stocking my pantry with great Mexican ingredients, and figuring out how to make these foods that were a part of me. Today she's older, but she still loves to keep me company in the *cocina*, dumping, mixing, pouring, stirring. But you honestly wouldn't be reading this without her pushing me. *¡Mi querida niña!*

I figured it was time to share my recipes with you because I feel so blessed and lucky to have my Mexican heritage and to have grown up with these rich, centuries-old traditions. To have my own family cookbook, if you will. But I know not everyone is so lucky, so I want to help.

In this book, I'm finally sharing the dishes I highlight in my videos, plus the food I cook at home for my family and friends. Many of these are Mexican classics from my grandmother by way of my mom, and let me tell you, it was no small task figuring out exact measurements! But I did it, and I'm passing that information on to you for the first time. I also included my own Mexican-inspired dishes, and even a couple that aren't Mexican. I love teaching my generation how to cook without being intimidated or scared, with a book that's easy to follow as I take you through the recipes step by simple step. These are delicious meals that will bring you and your family comfort, none of them too expensive or fancy.

My cookbook isn't all hot chiles and spiciness (though there is plenty of both to satisfy those cravings). The reality is that Mexican food is much more nuanced than you may realize, and everything's full of flavor, nurturing, and warmth. This is unpretentious food: authentic, cozy, and comfortable meals to make at home, helping you feel like you're with your family and creating new family traditions that connect us all through dishes like my viral My Mom's Ham and Cheese Spaghetti (page 76)—that spaghetti is so easy to make. It's the kind of dish that gets passed down, beginning the type of beloved generational thread we all want. Plus, it's *muy deliciosa!*

I also demystify the Mexican pantry. Don't know the difference between a serrano and a chipotle chile? I'll tell you! Some of these items may be new to you, but they're all things you can use in many ways in many different dishes, and they're all pretty easy to find in local markets these days (or you can order them online). Plus, I teach you a few simple cooking techniques to master that you'll use again and again.

My journey has taken me from being just a spectator in the kitchen to making it my happy place, because it's in the kitchen where I get to show my love of family, tradition, and heritage. And my family is totally on board. (Well, I'm always kicking Brandon out of the kitchen, but he truly is my biggest supporter.) From family meals to big gatherings, these recipes will help you master it all. Without stress, but with flavor—*con sabor*! I couldn't have done any of this without taking a look back, playing and experimenting, and, of course, getting encouragement from my darling Izzy.

ABOUT THIS BOOK

Welcome to my kitchen! This book reflects how I cook for my family and friends, balancing our busy lives with the joy of delicious meals.

In the *Desayuno / Breakfast* chapter, you'll find quick, authentic Mexican recipes for rush-out-the-door mornings and indulgent options for lazy weekends. Dinner is split into *Weeknight Dinners* for hectic days and *Weekend Dinners* for when you have time to savor the process. The *Antojitos y Acompañantes* section is a treasure trove of salads, starters, snacks, and sides, perfect for any occasion, from casual lunches to festive gatherings.

For your sweet tooth, *Desserts and Drinks* offers everything from simple treats to showstopping finales, along with sips to keep you warm or refreshed throughout the year.

Finally, the *Basics* chapter covers essential salsas and the secrets to perfect rice and beans, ensuring you have a strong foundation for your Mexican-cooking adventure.

Some overall notes:

- While I hope you'll make my homemade tortillas (page 222), store-bought 6-inch corn tortillas work well, too.

- Note that in a 10-inch pan, you will need 1 cup of oil for every ¼ inch of oil depth.

- Many recipes call for frying. I recommend using a 10-inch pan that is about 2 inches deep for shallow-frying. But when you need a greater depth of oil—anything over 3 to 4 cups of oil (a depth of about 1 inch)—you should use a Dutch oven or other deep, heavy-bottomed pot so that you have safe clearance between the oil level and the rim of the pot.

- I always have a pot of Frijoles de Edith (page 171) simmering to serve alongside most dishes. If you don't have time to make them from scratch, you can use store-bought refried beans.

MY MEXICAN KITCHEN ESSENTIALS

My cooking is a heartfelt celebration of my Mexican heritage and the meals I lovingly make for my family here in California. The recipes burst with bold flavors, featuring core ingredients like chiles, corn, beans, rice, cilantro, tomatoes, tomatillos, and Mexican cheeses. Some of these ingredients might be old friends to you; others might be new discoveries but are essential for these dishes. This is just the start of your cooking journey. I can't wait for you to make these dishes your own family favorites.

You can find the ingredients that follow in many Mexican markets or neighborhood grocery stores, or order them online. Substitutions are suggested in the Tip section of the recipes whenever possible.

Chile Peppers

Chile peppers are either fresh or dried, and depending on which type you use, they can lend many different flavors to a dish. Do you want something smoky or bright? Spicy or colorful? Gentle or bold? Chiles are a major part of everything from soups to stews to marinades, and, of course, are a key ingredient in salsa! Here are a few of the peppers I find myself using most often.

Fresh Chiles

These are the fresh chiles I use most often, in alphabetical order.

- **Anaheim peppers** are light green and relatively mild, with a fresh flavor. First grown in Anaheim, California, at the beginning of the twentieth century, they are 6 to 10 inches long. You'll find them in my Pozole Verde (page 104). They have a slightly smoky, sweet flavor and mild heat.

- **Jalapeños** are probably the most familiar and can vary in heat. Generally, the smaller ones tend to be hotter. I adore pickled jalapeños and always keep jars in my pantry for a snack of Botanas Mexicana con Cueritos (page 149). I also prefer pickled jalapeños to the usual fresh in my Favorite Guacamole (page 236).

- **Poblano peppers** are one of the most popular fresh chiles in Mexican cooking. They have a dark green color and mild flavor. They are most famous for being stuffed with meat or cheese and roasted (or deep-fried) for chiles rellenos poblanos, although my version (see page 123) uses potatoes and cheese for the stuffing. They're also crucial in my Salsa Verde (page 235), Spaghetti Verde (page 80), and many other recipes in this book. We also enjoy them roasted, cut into strips, and popped into a tortilla.

- **Serranos** are small, slim green peppers that are very hot—about three times hotter than a jalapeño! They are common in hot sauces and salsas like my Salsa Fresca (page 229) and Salsa Verde (page 235).

Dried Chiles

There are a million different dried chiles, so I've included the ones I use the most and that you'll need for the recipes in this book. You can find dried chiles in supermarkets, Mexican markets, and online. My favorite brand is El Guapo.

- **Ancho chiles** are dried poblanos with a hint of chocolate, raisin, and spice to their flavor. They add depth to Salsa Roja (page 225).

- **Chile de árbol** is the dried chile I reach for when I want bright spice in a soup, stew, or salsa (page 228). It's small but mighty and packs a lot of flavor in its slender red package.

- **Chipotle peppers** are dried, smoked jalapeños. One thing is for sure: Chipotles are a must-have flavor bomb! While you can sometimes find powdered chipotle in the spice aisle, they're most commonly used canned as chipotles in adobo sauce (common brands are La Costeña and Embasa).

The adobo they're packed in is a deep red, spicy, tangy sauce made of tomatoes and spices. After opening a can, transfer whatever chipotles and adobo you don't use to a small airtight container and refrigerate for up to 2 weeks. Remember that when I call for a specific number of chipotles in my recipes, I refer to how many chipotles are needed from one can— not the number of total cans!

- **Guajillos** are mild dried chiles, probably the second most commonly used chile after anchos. If you want a sauce to be red but not too spicy, guajillos are the chile for you. They're found in my Salsa Roja (page 225).

- **Pasillas** are another mainstay chile of my Mexican pantry. This richly flavored, slightly sweet, not-too-spicy dried chile is named for its dark, wrinkled skin (*pasilla* means "little raisin"). You'll find them in the sauce for both Mole con Pollo (page 139) and Quesabirria Tacos (page 118).

HOW TO PREP DRIED CHILES

Take your knife and chop off (and discard) the tough stem, then split the chile open to remove the dried seeds and pith. Recipes will often call for soaking dried chiles in boiling water to soften them up before blending, though sometimes you'll drop a whole one into a stew to extract flavor and a touch of spice (don't worry, you can take it out before serving to avoid an unpleasant surprise).

Mexican Dairy

Mexican dairy products are an essential part of making my *comida auténtica*. There are several different varieties of cheese, each with specific uses that bring something unique to the party. And then there is the one and only Mexican crema, our type of sour cream. The brand Los Altos is an excellent resource for fresh Mexican dairy products.

Cheese

- **Queso Cotija**, named for the town of Cotija, Michoacán, is an aged Mexican cheese made from cow's milk. It's a little salty, with a firm texture, and is often sold grated. It has Parmesan vibes and is great sprinkled on top of almost anything. It's a must on top of my Esquites (page 159).

- **Queso fresco** is mild, like panela, but a bit crumblier, like feta. Typically made from cow's or goat's milk, it adds texture and a nice jolt of freshness to dishes.

- **Queso Oaxaca** is a firm, low-fat Mexican cheese that melts beautifully, making it perfect for quesadillas. It has a texture like string cheese.

- **Queso panela** is a fresh (unaged) cow's-milk cheese that tastes like firm mozzarella. I like it because it doesn't melt, adding a nice textural element to soups. You can crumble it on top of enchiladas or bake it alone.

Cream

- **Crema Mexicana** is a silky, slightly tangy Mexican cream that resembles crème fraîche or sour cream, only thinner. I rely on crema Mexicana when making my pastas (pages 75–82) and to drizzle on tacos (page 83) and gorditas (page 133). If you can't find Mexican crema, you'll find the proportions for substituting a mix of sour cream and a bit of milk in Tips below the recipes that call for it throughout the book.

- **Media crema** is a canned cream, with a consistency halfway between evaporated milk and condensed milk. I haven't found the perfect substitute for media crema; you could try heavy cream, but the flavor will vary slightly.

Produce

Fresh produce is one of the most essential elements of authentic Mexican cooking, and every Mexican pantry needs a few specific items beyond lemons, limes, onions, and garlic.

- **Avocados** are the true heroes of Mexican cooking, and their delicious, creamy imprint is all over my food. I prefer the wrinkly dark green Hass variety. There's practically an avocado library in my kitchen, with one in every stage of ripeness almost always on hand. There are used in too many recipes to name here!

- **Chayote** is a member of the squash family. It is firm-fleshed, with a light sweetness, a taste somewhere between apple and cucumber, and the snap of jicama. It can be eaten raw (in salads) or lightly cooked, as it is in Izzy's Chicken Soup (page 58) and Caldo de Res (page 143). It also makes a great component of slaw.

- **Cilantro** provides an herbal, grassy, almost citrusy base to most of my recipes. I always use fresh cilantro, and most often only the leaves, not the stems. Please don't skip it if it's called for as a garnish.

- **Mexican squash**, sometimes called grey squash, looks like a fatter, lighter-green zucchini and has a slightly lighter flavor. It's the secret to my Guacamole Salsa Dupe (page 232), and is excellent fried, used as a veggie substitute for meat in tacos and burritos, or pureed to thicken soups and sauces or add bulk to stews. You can use green or yellow squash as a substitute if needed.

- **Tomatillos** are also known as Mexican husk tomatoes because of their easy-to-remove papery husks. They provide a hit of tang and citrus in Salsa Verde (page 235) and Costillas en Salsa (page 136), among other dishes. I char them with onions and garlic on my comal for a roasted sauce or blanch them for salsa verde. They can be very tricky: If you overcook them, they can turn sour on you, so pay attention!

- **Corn tortillas** are served at almost every meal in place of bread and are used to make countless dishes, including enchiladas (pages 91 and 92), tostadas (pages 116 and 129), tacos (pages 83, 86, and 118). I've shared my homemade recipe on page 222, but I can't lie—I'm not always in the mood! There are many high-quality store-bought corn (and flour) tortillas in my fridge for those days.

- **Dried pinto beans** are a daily need in my kitchen, and I almost always have a pot of them simmering (page 171). My trick is to skip the soaking and use a slow cooker so we can enjoy these at almost every dinner. I suggest using canned refried beans if you're tight on time.

- **Flour tortillas** are used less frequently, but are just as delicious. (My comfort food is a flour tortilla slathered with butter!) I've included a recipe for making your own (page 224), but again . . . no guilt for using store-bought.

- **Masa harina** (preferably Maseca brand) is an instant corn flour that is the foundation of any dish that relies on a tortilla or corn shell. Unlike plain cornmeal, the corn for masa harina is processed in a way that gives the flour a distinctive, toasted flavor. It's what you need to make your own soft Corn Tortillas (page 222), empanadas (page 121), and Sopes (page 130). Don't be intimidated; you'll get the hang of making your own in no time. It's also used as a thickener for soups and atole (page 219), a thick chocolate corn pudding.

- **Mexican chocolate** is usually sold in tablet form. It is a combination of chocolate, sugar, and cinnamon. This gives Mexican chocolate drinks their distinctive flavor. Ibarra is the brand I prefer.

- **Piloncillo** is a raw cane sugar from Latin America with a smoky caramel flavor that comes in a solid cone; to use it, you grate the amount you need from the cone. Piloncillo can be tricky to find in stores but is readily available online. The closest substitute would be dark brown sugar.

- **Rice** is a must for soaking up the delicious sauces from so many of these recipes. Golden Star Thai jasmine rice is nicely fragrant and fluffy, but any white rice will do for Arroz Blanco (page 164). My steaming method also works for classic Arroz Rojo (page 167) and Arroz Poblano (page 168).

Standard Pantry

Here are more common ingredients I always have on hand:

- **Bay leaves**
- **Black beans, dried or canned**
- **Bouillon powder: chicken and beef (preferably Knorr brand)**
- **Cloves, whole**
- **Cumin, ground**
- **Garlic powder**
- **Goya Sazón seasoning**
- **Morton's table salt (not kosher or sea salt)**
- **Oils: avocado, canola (or other neutral oil), and extra-virgin olive oil**
- **Onion powder**
- **Oregano, dried (the more fragrant Mexican variety if you can find it)**
- **Preground black pepper**
- **Sugar (Zulka Morena cane sugar is my pick)**

Equipment

- **Comal:** This round, smooth, flat griddle without sides is traditionally used to cook tortillas and quesadillas; char tomatillos, onions, and garlic; and reheat tortillas. It's a simple item, so there is no need for bells and whistles. It is just a nice flat surface made out of cast-iron or another material with some weight. A cast-iron skillet or griddle is a good substitute if you don't have a comal.

- **Concha cutter:** Used to imprint a swirl or spiral shell pattern on dough, this traditional Mexican stamp is handy for making Conchas (page 44) or bread rolls, but you can also use a small paring knife.

- **Molcajete:** The Mexican version of a mortar and pestle, a molcajete is often made of coarse-textured volcanic stone. It's the thing the waiter brings over when making guacamole tableside. The rough surface inside the mortar and the grinding pestle are perfect for crushing chiles or garlic. I use mine to get the ideal texture on roasted salsas like Salsa Roja (page 225) and Chile de Árbol Salsa (page 228).

- **Molinillo:** This traditional wooden (often decoratively carved) whisk is used in Latin America to mix beverages like hot chocolate or atole (page 219), a chocolate corn pudding. It's a nice item if you want one, but a regular whisk or spoon will also work.

- **Tortilla press:** Very handy if you make lots of tortillas. A tortilla press is usually made of cast iron, cast aluminum, or good old-fashioned wood—which I prefer. It's a tool designed to flatten balls of dough into evenly round tortillas, saving you lots of effort and time instead of rolling.

- **Tortilla warmer:** Tortillas can dry out quickly, and a warmer will keep them soft, supple, and ready to enjoy throughout the meal. Pick up the woven wicker type, round and perfectly sized to fit corn tortillas, at a local Mexican grocery store or online.

DESAYUNO

Huevos a la Mexicana

Huevos Rancheros

Chilaquiles

Migas

Salchichas con Huevos /
Hot Dogs with Eggs

Hot Cakes de Banana /
Banana Pancakes

Conchas /
Sweet Breads

Chicharrónes en Salsa /
Pork Rinds in Chile Sauce

Slow Cooker Carnitas

BREAKFAST

HUEVOS A LA MEXICANA

This recipe is my go-to for busy weekday mornings because it's easier to make than its cousin Huevos Rancheros (page 35), which I usually save for slower weekend mornings. Eggs are softly scrambled with fresh green jalapeños and red tomatoes to create flecks of color to match the colors of the Mexican flag. Make sure to remove the pan from the heat when the curds are glossy so they stay soft and don't dry out.

4 large eggs

Salt and ground black pepper

¼ cup canola or other neutral oil

¼ white onion, peeled and diced (about ¼ cup)

2 fresh jalapeños, finely chopped

2 garlic cloves, minced

1 ripe Roma (plum) tomato, diced

For Serving:

Crumbled queso fresco

Finely chopped fresh cilantro

Frijoles de Edith (page 171), warmed, or store-bought refried beans

Warm corn tortillas

In a medium bowl, whisk together the eggs and a pinch each of salt and black pepper until combined. Set aside.

Heat the oil in a large skillet over medium-low heat. Add the onion, jalapeños, and garlic and cook, stirring occasionally, until the onion is translucent and everything is softened, 5 to 7 minutes. Stir in the tomato and cook until they begin to release their juices, about 1 minute.

Pour the eggs into the pan and use a silicone spatula to scramble the eggs until they are fully cooked and not runny, 2 to 3 minutes.

Evenly divide the eggs among four plates. Sprinkle with some queso fresco and garnish with cilantro. Serve with beans and warm tortillas.

HUEVOS RANCHEROS

Serves 2

Total time: 20 minutes

Huevos rancheros is a hearty breakfast created to satisfy hungry *rancheros* (ranchers) in Mexico, and it's what my abuela made for us on summer mornings at her ranch in Guanajuato. You start with a warm tortilla, then add a generous spoonful of my pinto beans, top them with a fried egg with a gooey yolk, and finish with a splash of salsa. Sometimes I double the beans and salsa for an easy dinner.

5 tablespoons canola or other neutral oil

3 ripe Roma (plum) tomatoes, diced

½ cup tomato sauce

⅓ cup finely chopped fresh cilantro

¼ white onion, peeled and diced (about ¼ cup)

1 fresh jalapeño, finely chopped

1 garlic clove, minced

¼ teaspoon ground cumin

¼ teaspoon dried oregano

Salt

2 large eggs

For Serving:

2 corn tortillas, warmed

2 cups mashed Frijoles de Edith (page 171), warmed, or store-bought refried beans

Crumbled queso fresco

Heat 3 tablespoons of the oil in a large skillet over medium heat. Add the diced tomatoes, tomato sauce, cilantro, onion, jalapeño, garlic, cumin, and oregano. Season with salt to taste. Cook, stirring occasionally, until the tomatoes release their juices and the onion becomes translucent, about 7 minutes.

Transfer the mixture to a blender (or food processor). With the steam vent in the blender top open, blend on high until creamy, about 45 seconds. Set aside.

Wipe the skillet clean, return it to the stove, and heat the remaining 2 tablespoons oil over medium-high heat. Add the eggs and cook until the whites are just set but the yolks are still runny, 3 to 4 minutes.

Place a tortilla on each plate. Spread the mashed beans evenly over the tortillas and top each with a fried egg. Spoon the tomato salsa on top of the eggs. Sprinkle with queso fresco and serve.

COCINA TIP:

- I use a bit more oil because I like my fried eggs to be extra crispy on the edges. You can use 1 tablespoon if you prefer the edges to be softer.

CHILAQUILES

Serves 4   *Total time: 45 minutes*

This is one of my favorite breakfasts to make for my husband, Brandon. It's his comfort food. Home-fried or store-bought tortilla chips are simmered in a homemade guajillo salsa just to the point where they are softened up but still have a bit of crunch, then finished with fried eggs. The garnishes—chopped fresh cilantro, queso blanco, homemade pickled onions, and a dollop of sour cream—take this dish from good to great.

10 dried New Mexico or guajillo chiles, stemmed, split, and seeded

2 ripe Roma (plum) tomatoes

1½ cups canola or other neutral oil

18 corn tortillas, cut into wedges

½ white onion, peeled and thinly sliced (about ½ cup)

2 garlic cloves, peeled but whole

1 tablespoon chicken bouillon powder, preferably Knorr

4 large eggs

Salt

For Serving:
Sour cream
Crumbled queso fresco
Chopped fresh cilantro
Pickled Onions (page 239)

COCINA TIP:

- You can fry the tortilla chips ahead of time and store them in a metal bowl covered with foil. You can also use store-bought tortilla chips.

Fill a large pot halfway with water and stir in the chiles and tomatoes. Bring to a boil over medium heat, and cook, stirring occasionally, until the chiles have softened, about 10 minutes.

Drain the chiles and tomatoes and set aside to cool slightly.

Set a wire rack over a baking sheet and have it near the stove. Heat 1 cup of the oil in a large high-sided pan over medium heat until hot. To check that the oil is hot enough for frying, dip a wooden toothpick in the oil; if the oil bubbles, it's ready. Working in batches to avoid crowding the pan, carefully add the tortilla wedges and fry until golden brown and crispy on both sides, using tongs or a slotted spoon to flip them, 2 to 3 minutes per side. Transfer the tortilla chips to the wire rack to cool and repeat with the remaining tortilla wedges.

In a blender, combine the cooled chiles and tomatoes, the onion, garlic, bouillon powder, and ½ cup water. Blend on high until the salsa is smooth, about 45 seconds.

Heat 2 tablespoons of the oil in a large skillet over medium heat. Pour in the salsa and bring to a simmer. Cook, stirring occasionally, until the salsa thickens slightly and the flavors meld, about 10 minutes. Add the tortilla chips and, using a spoon, mix until evenly combined. Transfer the mixture to a medium bowl and cover to keep warm.

Wipe the skillet clean. Heat the remaining 6 tablespoons of oil in the skillet over medium-high heat. Add the eggs, season with salt, and cook until the whites are just set but the yolks are still runny, 3 to 4 minutes.

Evenly divide the salsa and tortilla chips among four bowls. Place one egg on top of each dish. Top with some sour cream, queso fresco, cilantro, and pickled onions and serve.

MIGAS

This is for the scrambled egg crowd and comes together more quickly than Chilaquiles (page 36). Crispy tortillas are added to a warm salsa, along with the eggs, and cooked just until soft curds form for a delish mix of spice, crunch, and softness. My daughter, Izzy, loves my migas and eats them with her fingers like a plate of nachos!

1 cup canola or other neutral oil, for frying

15 corn or flour tortillas, cut into wedges or 1-inch-wide strips

3 ripe Roma (plum) tomatoes, diced

½ white onion, peeled and diced (about ½ cup)

2 fresh jalapeños, finely chopped

2 garlic cloves, minced

4 large eggs, beaten

Salt

For Serving:

2 cups mashed Frijoles de Edith (page 171), warmed, or store-bought refried beans

Salsa Verde (page 235) or Salsa Roja (page 225)

Crumbled queso fresco

Set a wire rack on a baking sheet and have it near the stove. Heat the oil in a large high-sided pan over medium heat until hot. To check that the oil is hot enough for frying, dip a wooden toothpick in the oil; if the oil bubbles, it's ready. Working in batches to avoid crowding the pan, carefully add the tortilla wedges and fry until golden brown and crispy, using tongs or a slotted spoon to flip them halfway, 2 to 3 minutes per side. Transfer the tortilla chips to the wire rack to cool and repeat with the remaining tortilla wedges.

Carefully discard all but 2 tablespoons of the oil from the skillet. Add the tomatoes, onion, jalapeños, and garlic and cook over medium heat, stirring occasionally, until the onion is translucent and the tomatoes release their juices, about 7 minutes. Stir in the tortilla chips.

Pour the eggs into the pan and season with salt to taste. Cook, stirring constantly with a silicone spatula, until the eggs are cooked through and no longer runny, about 3 minutes.

Evenly divide the eggs and beans among four plates. Top with salsa and garnish with queso fresco and serve.

COCINA TIP:

- You can also make these with store-bought tortilla chips.

HOT DOGS WITH EGGS

Serves 4   *Total time: 15 minutes*

Salchichas con huevos was a regular dish in my mom's rotation when we were growing up. They were her American spin on the traditional octopus sausages she grew up eating on the ranch. I have fond memories of her feeding them to my younger brothers when they were introduced to solid foods as babies (don't worry, she cut the hot dogs into small pieces so it was easy for a kid to eat safely!). Now, a generation later, Izzy adores them, especially with ketchup (of course).

¼ cup canola or other neutral oil
5 hot dogs, cut into 1-inch pieces
4 large eggs
Salt and ground black pepper
Warm corn or flour tortillas or sliced bread, for serving

Heat the oil in a large skillet over medium heat. Add the hot dogs and cook, stirring occasionally, until there are char marks on all sides, about 4 minutes.

Meanwhile, in a medium bowl, whisk the eggs with a pinch each of salt and black pepper until combined.

Reduce the heat to low. Pour the eggs into the pan and cook, stirring constantly with a silicone spatula, until the eggs are fully cooked and no longer runny, 2 to 3 minutes.

Evenly divide the egg mixture among four plates and serve with warm tortillas or between slices of bread.

BANANA PANCAKES

Serves 2   *Total time: 25 minutes*

These pancakes have quickly become a Saturday-morning breakfast tradition with my daughter. She loves to help prep the ingredients and watch me flip these sweet, moist pancakes. My trick of blending old-fashioned rolled oats with the banana adds fiber and creates the best texture. The caramelized bits of banana are my favorite part.

1 cup old-fashioned rolled oats
1 teaspoon baking powder
1 teaspoon granulated sugar
½ teaspoon baking soda
½ teaspoon salt
¼ teaspoon ground cinnamon
1 ripe banana, mashed
⅔ cup whole milk
1 large egg, at room temperature
2 tablespoons unsalted butter, plus more as needed

For Serving:
Berries
Maple syrup
Whipped cream
Powdered sugar

In a blender, combine the oats, baking powder, granulated sugar, baking soda, salt, and cinnamon and blend until evenly combined, about 1 minute. Add the banana, milk, and egg and blend until smooth, about 1 minute.

Melt the butter in a large skillet over medium heat. When it begins to bubble, use a ladle or large spoon to pour in enough batter for a 4-inch pancake. Cook until bubbles start to form on the top and the sides and the bottom begins to firm up, 3 to 4 minutes.

Flip the pancake and cook until lightly golden brown, 1 to 2 minutes. Transfer the pancake to platter and cover to keep warm. Repeat with the rest of the batter, adding more butter to the pan as needed.

Serve 2 pancakes per person, topped with berries, maple syrup, whipped cream, and a little powdered sugar!

SWEET BREADS

*Serves 4 to 6
(8 conchas)*

*Total time: 2 hours,
plus rising time*

These sweet and fluffy breads tantalize you from every Mexican *panadería* (bakery) window. They get their name from the *concha* (shell) pattern on the top of each loaf. My mother always brought some home on Sunday nights, so you can imagine how hard it was to wait through the whole weekend for these treats! That's one reason I came up with this recipe: Now I can have them whenever I crave them. They're topped with different flavors for a crunchy crust—traditionally white (granulated) sugar, cinnamon, orange, and even Oreo. I can't resist the chocolate. The conchas are extra yummy with coffee, hot chocolate, or Atole Chocolate (page 219). I usually use a stand mixer fitted with a dough hook to make these, but your two hands work just as well, and that's the way my mom made them. These take a lot of time, but are SO worth it. They're also fun to make with your kids. Serve them with Mexican hot chocolate (page 203).

Dough:

8 tablespoons (1 stick) unsalted butter, at room temperature, plus more for greasing

½ cup plus 1 teaspoon granulated sugar

½ cup whole milk, heated to about 110°F

1 (¼-ounce) packet instant yeast (2¼ teaspoons)

3¼ cups all-purpose flour, plus more if needed

1½ teaspoons ground cinnamon, or ½ stick cinnamon, freshly ground (see Tips)

1 teaspoon baking powder

3 large eggs, at room temperature

1 tablespoon vanilla extract

¼ teaspoon salt

Concha Crust:

1 cup all-purpose flour

½ cup powdered sugar

1 cup (1 stick) shortening

1 teaspoon vanilla extract

3 tablespoons unsalted softened butter, or more as needed for buttering

Make the dough:

Lightly grease a large bowl with butter. Grease a large baking sheet with butter.

In the bowl of a stand mixer fitted with the paddle attachment (or in a large bowl using a handheld mixer), whisk together 1 teaspoon of the granulated sugar, the milk, and yeast until combined. Let stand until bubbles appear, about 10 minutes (this is how you know your yeast is active and that the dough will rise).

Meanwhile, in a medium bowl, whisk together the flour, cinnamon, and baking powder until evenly combined.

To the bowl with the yeast mixture, add the butter, eggs, remaining ½ cup granulated sugar, the vanilla, and salt and beat on medium speed until smooth, about 3 minutes. Reduce the speed to low and slowly add the flour mixture and mix until a rough dough comes together, 10 to 15 minutes. Switch to the dough hook and knead on medium speed until smooth, about 20 minutes. If the dough is too sticky to handle, add more flour, 1 tablespoon at a time.

RECIPE CONTINUES

Transfer the dough to a lightly floured surface and knead with your hands until smooth, about 10 minutes. Transfer the dough to the greased bowl, cover with plastic wrap or a kitchen towel, and let rise in a warm spot (I use the inside of my oven) until doubled in size, 2 to 4 hours (see Tips).

Remove the dough from the bowl, transfer it to a lightly floured surface, and knead until smooth, about 4 minutes. Divide the dough into 8 equal portions and roll each portion into a ball, rolling until the little circle on the bottom of the roll disappears and the ball is totally smooth. Transfer the rolls to the prepared baking sheet and cover with a kitchen towel so they don't dry out while you make the concha crust.

Make the concha crust:
In a large bowl, combine the flour, powdered sugar, shortening, and vanilla and use your hands to mash into a smooth paste. Divide the paste into 8 equal portions and roll each portion into a ball. Line a tortilla press on both sides with plastic wrap so the paste doesn't stick. Place a ball of paste in the center and flatten it into a 6-inch disc. Remove the disc from the press using the bottom piece of plastic wrap. Reline the press and continue pressing the remaining crust dough. (Alternatively, use a rolling pin to roll the balls into rounds as thin as a 6-inch tortilla.)

Using your fingertips, lightly butter the top of each roll. (For a crunchier crust, use the same amount of shortening instead of the butter.) Carefully drape a concha crust disc on top of each buttered roll. Using a small knife, carefully make slits in each concha crust to mimic the lines of a seashell, taking care not to slice too deeply. Lightly cover the conchas with plastic wrap or a kitchen towel and let rise until doubled in size, 30 to 45 minutes.

Meanwhile, preheat the oven to 350°F.

Bake for 18 to 22 minutes, until the conchas have doubled in size and the bottoms are golden. Remove from the oven and set the baking sheet on a wire rack. Let the conchas cool for 15 to 20 minutes. Serve warm.

COCINA TIPS:

- I prefer to grind my own cinnamon in a spice grinder whenever possible for the freshest flavor.

- The proofing time depends on the room temperature. If your kitchen is warmer, the yeast may proof more rapidly.

- To reheat leftover conchas (if you have any!), wrap them individually in a damp paper towel and microwave for 15 seconds.

PORK RINDS IN CHILE SAUCE

Serves 4   *Total time: 30 minutes*

Most Americans don't think of this as breakfast food, but it's a true Sunday-morning Mexican family breakfast dish in our home. My favorite thing about this is how the fried pork rinds become soft and juicy from the tangy salsa. The leftovers (if there are any) make flavorful tacos.

4 tablespoons canola or other neutral oil

1 pound tomatillos, husked and rinsed (see Tips)

1 white onion, peeled

4 garlic cloves, peeled but whole

3 fresh serrano chiles, stemmed

1 cup fresh cilantro, plus more for garnish

1 tablespoon chicken bouillon powder, preferably Knorr

½ teaspoon salt

½ teaspoon ground black pepper

⅛ teaspoon ground cumin

8 ounces chicharrónes (fried pork rinds)

Warm corn tortillas, for serving

Frijoles de Edith (page 171), warmed, or store-bought refried beans, for serving

Heat 1 tablespoon of the oil in a large skillet over medium-high heat. Carefully add the tomatillos, onion, garlic, and serranos and cook, constantly moving them around using tongs or a wooden spoon, until charred and softened, about 15 minutes. Transfer the vegetables to a blender and add the cilantro, bouillon powder, salt, black pepper, and cumin. With the steam vent in the top open, blend until the salsa is smooth, about 1 minute.

In the same skillet you used for the vegetables, heat the remaining 3 tablespoons oil over medium heat. Pour the salsa into the pan and simmer, stirring occasionally, until it thickens and reduces slightly, about 10 minutes. Stir in the pork rinds and cook, stirring occasionally, until softened, about 2 minutes.

Evenly divide the pork rinds among four bowls. Serve with warm corn tortillas and beans, garnished with cilantro.

COCINA TIPS:

- To clean tomatillos, first remove the outer husk, then thoroughly clean with cool water and fruit and veggie wash or natural dish soap to remove the sticky residue.

- You can use any leftovers with fried or scrambled eggs for a quick, easy, and tasty breakfast.

SLOW COOKER CARNITAS

Serves 6 to 8

Total time: 15 minutes, plus 6 to 8 hours in a slow cooker or 3½ to 4 hours in the oven

This Sunday-brunch dish is put together on Saturday in the slow cooker and left to simmer overnight. Nothing is better than waking up to the aroma of carnitas! It's not quite the typical Mexican recipe, but I think you'll appreciate my suggestion to squeeze the softened garlic out of the skins back into the pot to flavor the pork. Serve with either store-bought or my Favorite Guacamole (page 236).

3 to 4 pounds boneless pork shoulder or butt, trimmed of excess fat and cut into 3- to 4-inch cubes

2 teaspoons salt

1 teaspoon chili powder

1 teaspoon ground cumin

1 teaspoon dried oregano

½ teaspoon ground black pepper

1 head garlic, top one-third sliced off to expose the cloves

½ white onion, peeled

3 bay leaves

2 fresh rosemary sprigs

2 fresh thyme sprigs

1 cup chicken broth

1 cup orange juice

Juice of 1 lime

For Serving:

Warm corn tortillas

Edith's Favorite Guacamole (page 236)

Sliced onion

Roughly chopped fresh cilantro

Pat the pork dry. In a large bowl, whisk together the salt, chili powder, cumin, oregano, and black pepper until evenly combined. Add the pork to the spice mixture and use your hands or a large spoon to toss until the pork is evenly coated. Place the pork in a 6-quart slow cooker. Scatter the garlic, onion, bay leaves, rosemary, and thyme on top of the pork.

In a large measuring cup, whisk together the broth, orange juice, and lime juice. Pour the broth mixture into the slow cooker. With a large spoon, carefully turn the pork chunks to combine the ingredients and evenly coat the pork with the liquid. Cover and cook on low for 8 hours or on high for 6 hours, until the pork is tender and shreds easily with a fork.

Carefully remove and discard the bay leaves and herb stems. Remove the garlic head and set aside. Using two forks, shred the pork directly in the slow cooker.

Use a large spoon to mix the pork and juices, coating the meat evenly. If desired, squeeze the softened garlic cloves out of the skins into the pot with the pork and mix well.

Evenly divide the stew among bowls. Serve with warm tortillas, guacamole, onion, and cilantro.

COCINA TIP:

- If you don't have a slow cooker, you can cook the carnitas in a Dutch oven or a large lidded pot in the oven instead: Preheat the oven to 325°F. Assemble all the ingredients in the Dutch oven or pot as directed and bake for 3½ to 4 hours, until the meat is tender and shreds easily with a fork, stirring midway through.

CENAS ENTRE SEMANA

Pollo Asado

Sopa de Fideo

Caldo de Pollo /
Izzy's Chicken Soup

Sopa de Queso con Papas

Caldo de Albóndigas /
Meatball Soup

Carne en su Jugo / *Beef Stew
in Spicy Tomatillo Sauce*

Ensalada de Jaiva /
Imitation Crab Salad

Cóctel de Camarones de Papá /
Dad's Shrimp Cocktail

Ensalada de Atún / *Tuna Salad*

Chicken with Alfredo Pasta

My Mom's Ham and
Cheese Spaghetti

Brandon's Shrimp Pasta

Spaghetti Verde / *Spaghetti with
Poblano Chili Sauce*

Tacos de Papa

Tacos de Camarones

Enchiladas Rojas

Enchiladas Verdes

Fried Quesadillas

Chicken Marsala

Pollo a la Chipotle

Pollo en Chile Guajillo

Pozole Verde

Milanesa de Res o Pollo /
Beef or Chicken Cutlet

Carne Asada

Bistec a la Mexicana

Mexican Corn Dogs

WEEKNIGHT
DINNERS

POLLO ASADO

I'm proud of this recipe because I devised a technique to deliver the juiciest chicken. I spatchcock it, a fancy word for cutting out the backbone so the bird can be flattened. This guarantees that your chicken will cook evenly, which means no dry breasts! A steady hand and some sturdy kitchen shears are all the tools you need. Marinate the chicken the night before in the guajillo and chile de árbol marinade, and then it's up to you whether to fire up the grill or roast it in the oven. The meat is so tender, it just falls off the bone.

4 dried guajillo chiles, stemmed, split, and seeded

½ small white onion, peeled and roughly chopped (about ⅓ cup)

6 garlic cloves, peeled but whole

3 dried chiles de árbol, stemmed, split, and seeded

Juice of ½ orange

Juice of 1 lime

1 tablespoon white wine vinegar

2 (1.41-ounce) packages Goya Sazón seasoning

2 tablespoons Lawry's casero pollo asada seasoning

1 tablespoon ground black pepper, plus more as needed

1 teaspoon dried oregano

1 teaspoon salt, plus more as needed

1 (3- to 4-pound) whole chicken, spatchcocked (see Tip)

Canola or other neutral oil, for the grill

The night before you want to cook the chicken, place the guajillo chiles in a small pot with enough water to cover. Bring to a boil over medium heat and cook until the chiles soften, about 5 minutes.

Using a slotted spoon, transfer the guajillos to a blender. Add the onion, garlic, chiles de árbol, orange juice, lime juice, vinegar, Sazón, pollo asada seasoning, black pepper, oregano, and salt and blend on high until smooth, about 45 seconds.

Place the chicken in a large baking dish and season it all over with black pepper and salt. Pour the marinade over the chicken and use a spatula or your hands to spread it evenly. Cover with plastic wrap and refrigerate overnight or for 12 to 24 hours before grilling or roasting.

Arroz Blanco (page 164)

Frijoles de Edith (page 171), warmed, or store-bought refried beans

Edith's Favorite Guacamole (page 236) or store-bought

To grill:

The next day, heat a grill to 350°F. Lightly oil the grates and place the chicken on the grill, skin-side down. Cover and grill for 45 minutes. Using tongs, flip the chicken and cook, covered, until the skin is crispy and the internal temperature registers 165°F, about 35 minutes more. Transfer the chicken to a plate to rest for at least 20 minutes before carving and serving.

Arrange the chicken pieces on a large platter. Serve with bowls of rice, beans, and guacamole.

COCINA TIPS:

- To spatchcock a chicken, set it on a cutting board breast-side down. With a pair of sturdy poultry or kitchen shears, cut along one side of the backbone from neck to tail. Repeat on the other side of the backbone and pull out the back. Flip the chicken over and press down hard on the breastbone at the neck end to flatten the bird as much as you can.

- To roast: Preheat the oven to 450°F. Place the chicken breast side up in a lightly oiled roasting pan and roast for 50 to 60 minutes, until the internal temperature registers 165°F. Remove the chicken from the oven and let it rest for at least 20 minutes before carving and serving.

SOPA DE FIDEO

Serves 4 to 6   *Total time: 20 minutes*

Comforting on a cold winter day and essential if you have a cold or the flu, this soup is what my mother stirred up to get us healthy. I promise this sopa de fideo will nourish and bring you back to life in almost any situation! Fideo is short thin pasta, but if you can't find it, just break thin pasta, such as vermicelli or angel hair, into short pieces.

4 ripe Roma (plum) tomatoes, diced

½ small white onion, peeled and diced (about ⅓ cup)

¼ green bell pepper, diced

2 garlic cloves, peeled but whole

1 (1.41-ounce) package Goya Sazón seasoning (optional)

2 tablespoons chicken bouillon powder, preferably Knorr, or more as needed

⅛ teaspoon ground cumin

Salt

⅓ cup canola or other neutral oil

7 ounces fideo noodles or broken vermicelli, angel hair pasta, or spaghetti

Juice of 1 lemon

For Serving:

Hot sauce

Crumbled queso fresco or feta cheese

Finely chopped fresh cilantro, for garnish

In a blender (or food processor), combine the tomatoes, onion, bell pepper, garlic, Sazón (if using), bouillon powder, cumin, a pinch of salt, and 3 cups water and blend until very smooth, about 45 seconds. Add more water as needed for a smooth salsa.

Heat the oil in a medium pot over medium heat. Add the fideo and cook, stirring constantly, until golden brown and toasted, about 2 minutes. Pour the blitzed tomato mixture into the pot, bring to a boil, and cook, stirring occasionally, until thickened, 10 to 15 minutes. Stir in the lemon juice.

Evenly divide the soup among bowls. Top with a dash of hot sauce and a sprinkle of queso fresco, garnish with fresh chopped cilantro, and serve.

COCINA TIP:

• For a smooth and silky broth, strain the tomato mixture after blending.

IZZY'S CHICKEN SOUP

Serves 8

Total time: 1 hour 30 minutes

Every culture has a version of chicken soup, because it seems to cure everything. My abuela would make this recipe for us on the ranch, and I love, love, love it! My mom kept up the tradition and made this nonstop—because even on hot summer days, we kids would eat it. That's how irresistible, comforting, and—bonus—enriching this soup is. It makes me so proud that it's now Izzy's favorite, so I've officially renamed it, and I can't wait for her to learn this recipe so she can continue the tradition.

6 chicken drumsticks, skin removed (see Tips)

4 bone-in, skinless chicken thighs

1 head garlic, top one-third sliced off to expose the cloves

½ white onion, peeled

2 bay leaves

1 tablespoon chicken bouillon powder, preferably Knorr

Salt and ground black pepper

1 ear corn, husked and cut into 4 pieces

4 large carrots, peeled, cut into 4 pieces

1 large or 2 small russet potatoes, cut into large chunks

2 medium chayote squash (about 1 pound total), peeled, seeded, and cut into large chunks

2 medium Mexican squash or zucchini, cut into large chunks

¾ cup finely chopped fresh cilantro

Arroz Rojo (page 167), for serving

Lime wedges

In a large stockpot, combine 3 quarts (12 cups) water, the chicken drumsticks, chicken thighs, garlic, onion, bay leaves, and bouillon powder. Cover and bring to a boil over medium heat. Reduce the heat to medium-low and simmer, uncovered, regularly skimming the foam from the top, until the chicken is tender and the liquid has reduced, about 45 minutes. Season with salt and pepper to taste.

Pour 2 cups water into the pot. Add the corn and cook until just tender, about 4 minutes. Add the carrots and cook for 4 minutes, just to give them a head start. Stir in the potatoes, chayote, Mexican squash, and cilantro. Increase the heat to high and bring to a boil. Reduce the heat to medium-low, cover, and simmer until the vegetables are tender, about 30 minutes. Taste and adjust the seasoning.

Discard the bay leaves. Remove the head of garlic from the pot and, if desired, squeeze the garlic cloves from the skins into the broth and stir to incorporate. Using tongs, carefully remove the chicken pieces from the pot and transfer to a bowl until cool enough to handle, then pull the chicken meat off the bones.

Divide the chicken evenly among eight bowls. Ladle the broth and vegetables into the bowls. Serve with rice and with lime wedges for squeezing.

COCINA TIPS:

- If you don't want to remove the chicken skin from the drumsticks, the soup will have much more fat. You can either remove the fat while skimming or chill the soup until the fat hardens for easier removal.

- Don't skip the skimming step. It keeps the soup clear instead of cloudy.

SOPA DE QUESO CON PAPAS

Serves 4 or 5

Total time: 30 minutes

This soup, another childhood fave, has a luscious and creamy texture that is so comforting and beyond delicious. My brothers and I love the way the smoky roasted poblanos and the sharpness of the cheese play off of each other. It's a filling and budget-friendly—but never boring—main dish.

3 fresh poblano chiles

3 ripe Roma (plum) tomatoes, roughly chopped

½ white onion, peeled and roughly chopped, (about ½ cup)

2 garlic cloves, peeled but whole

1 tablespoon Knorr Tomato Bouillon with Chicken Flavor powder

1 teaspoon ground black pepper

1 teaspoon dried oregano

⅓ cup canola or other neutral oil

3 White Rose potatoes, new potatoes, or any other waxy potato (about 1 pound total), peeled and cut into 1-inch cubes

1 (10-ounce) package queso panela or queso fresco, cubed

1 cup heavy cream

¼ cup finely chopped fresh cilantro

Salt (optional)

Heat a large dry skillet over medium heat. Add the poblanos and cook, using tongs to turn, until they are charred on all sides, about 5 minutes per side. (Alternatively, place on a baking sheet and broil until the skins start to blacken, about 5 minutes per side.) Transfer the chiles to a large bowl, cover with a kitchen towel, and let steam for about 5 minutes. Carefully remove the chiles from the bowl and set aside until cool enough to handle, then peel them and discard the skin, stems, and seeds. Cut the peppers into thin strips and set aside.

In a blender, combine the tomatoes, onion, garlic, bouillon powder, black pepper, and oregano and blend on high until smooth, about 45 seconds.

Heat the oil in a Dutch oven or large pot over medium-low heat for 2 minutes. Add the tomato mixture along with 1½ cups water and bring to a boil over medium heat. Reduce the heat to low and simmer, stirring occasionally, for 10 minutes to meld the flavors.

Stir in the potatoes, queso, and cream and cook, stirring occasionally, until the potatoes are fork-tender, about 15 minutes.

Stir the poblano strips and cilantro into the soup. Taste and season with salt, if necessary.

Divide the soup evenly among bowls. Serve immediately.

COCINA TIP:

- If you can't find the tomato-flavored bouillon, use regular chicken bouillon powder and add 1 teaspoon tomato paste.

MEATBALL SOUP

Serves 6 to 8

Total time: 45 minutes

This meatball soup is hearty and healthy and simmers on my stove all winter. Adding shredded zucchini to the meatballs is a secret way to sneak in more veggies, and the robust tomato broth is brimming with carrots, potatoes, celery, squash, and chipotles. One clever trick I swear by is to mix uncooked rice into the meatballs. As they simmer, the rice cooks and absorbs all the flavors, and you save a step.

Meatballs:

1½ pounds lean ground beef (93 % lean)

½ cup uncooked extra-long-grain white rice, preferably Mahatma

½ cup finely chopped Mexican squash (see Tips), zucchini, or yellow squash

½ cup finely chopped fresh cilantro

¼ white onion, peeled and finely chopped (about ¼ cup)

2 garlic cloves, minced

2 large eggs, lightly beaten

1 teaspoon garlic powder

1 teaspoon onion powder

1 teaspoon dried oregano

1 teaspoon ground black pepper

½ teaspoon salt

Tomato Sauce:

5 ripe Roma (plum) tomatoes, quartered

¼ green bell pepper, sliced

¼ white onion, peeled and sliced (about ¼ cup)

2 garlic cloves, peeled but whole

1 (1.41-ounce) packet Goya Sazón seasoning

1 tablespoon chicken bouillon powder, preferably Knorr

¼ teaspoon ground cumin

Make the meatballs:

In a large bowl, combine the ground beef, rice, squash, cilantro, onion, garlic, eggs, garlic powder, onion powder, oregano, black pepper, and salt and mix with your hands until evenly combined. Form into 2-inch balls (about the size of a golf ball) and place them on a baking sheet. Refrigerate while you make the sauce.

Make the tomato sauce:

In a blender, combine the tomatoes, bell pepper, onion, garlic, Sazón, bouillon powder, cumin, and 3 cups water and blend until smooth, about 45 seconds.

Caldo:

½ teaspoon salt, plus more
as needed

4 celery stalks, cut into
¼-inch-thick slices

3 medium carrots, peeled and
sliced into ¼-inch-thick rounds

3 medium russet potatoes,
peeled and diced

2 medium Mexican squash or
zucchini, halved lengthwise and
cut crosswise into ¼-inch-thick
half-moons

1 cup fresh cilantro, roughly
chopped

2 chipotle peppers from canned
chipotles in adobo sauce

Arroz Blanco (page 164),
for serving (optional)

Make the caldo:

Pour the tomato sauce into a large
pot. Add the salt and 2 cups water
and bring to a boil over medium
heat. Add the meatballs, reduce
the heat to low, and simmer, stirring
occasionally, until the meatballs
are cooked through, about
25 minutes.

Add the celery, carrots, potatoes,
squash, cilantro, and chipotles
and gently stir from the bottom to
incorporate the vegetables so that
you don't break up the meatballs.
Bring to a boil over high heat, then
reduce the heat to medium-low
and simmer, stirring occasionally,
until the potatoes are fork-tender,
about 15 minutes. Taste and season
with more salt.

Evenly divide the soup among
bowls and serve with rice, if desired.

COCINA TIPS:

- If you don't eat red meat,
  substitute ground turkey or
  chicken for the beef.

- Mexican squash is firmer and
  sweeter than regular zucchini,
  so if I'm using zucchini, I
  sometimes add a pinch of
  sugar.

BEEF STEW IN SPICY TOMATILLO SAUCE

Serves 6

Total time: 1 hour

This is a superhero stew. It's packed with bacon, steak, and pinto beans simmered in salsa verde, a green sauce bright with tomatillos and some tingly heat from the serrano chiles. Just don't overcook the tomatillos or the sauce will be too sour. Make a big batch to last the week, because it tastes even better the next day!

Sauce:

5 fresh serrano chiles, stemmed

16 tomatillos, husked and rinsed (see Tips on page 47)

2 cups low-sodium chicken broth or water

2 cups fresh cilantro leaves with 2-inch stems

½ small white onion, peeled

4 garlic cloves, peeled but whole

1½ tablespoons chicken bouillon powder, preferably Knorr

Salt and ground black pepper

Carne:

1 pound bacon, cut crosswise into 1-inch-wide strips

6 scallions

5 fresh güero chiles (see Tips)

3 tablespoons canola or other neutral oil

2 pounds carne ranchera (see Tips) or skirt steak, cut into thin strips

Salt and ground black pepper

2½ cups Frijoles de Edith (page 171), warmed, or canned pinto beans (drained and rinsed, if canned)

For Serving:

Roughly chopped fresh cilantro

Roughly chopped white onion

Lime wedges

Make the sauce:

Bring a medium pot of water to a boil over medium heat. Add the serranos, reduce the heat to low, and simmer until the chiles soften, about 4 minutes. Add the tomatillos and cook until they turn a brownish-yellow color, about 5 minutes. Drain the chiles and tomatillos and let cool slightly.

Transfer the chiles and tomatillos to a blender and add the broth, cilantro, onion, garlic, bouillon powder, and a pinch of each of salt and black pepper. With the steam vent in the blender top open, blend on high until smooth, about 45 seconds. Set the sauce aside.

Make the carne:

Heat a large skillet over medium heat. Add the bacon and cook, stirring occasionally, until golden brown and crispy, about 6 minutes. Add the scallions and whole güero chiles and cook, stirring occasionally, until charred and softened, about 3 minutes. Using a slotted spoon, transfer the bacon mixture to a heatproof

bowl. Discard all but ⅓ cup of the rendered bacon fat.

Return the skillet to medium heat and add the oil. Add the beef and season with a big pinch each of salt and black pepper. Cook, stirring occasionally, until slightly charred, golden brown, and cooked through, about 15 minutes.

Add the sauce, beans, and bacon mixture and mix until evenly combined. Simmer, stirring occasionally, until thickened, about 25 minutes.

Divide the stew evenly among six bowls. Top with cilantro and onion. Serve with lime wedges for squeezing.

COCINA TIPS:

- Carne ranchera is known by a few names, including flap meat, flap steak, bavette, and bottom sirloin flap.

- Fresh güero chiles may be tricky to find. You can substitute the same amount of fresh jalapeño.

IMITATION CRAB SALAD

Serves 6

Total time: 20 minutes, plus 2 to 4 hours marinating time

This salad is similar to a ceviche, where the acid from the lime marinade "cooks" the fish. In our family, it's always made with imitation crab or surimi, and gets its zesty kick from the Clamato, lime, and fresh jalapeños. I make this during the blazing hot summer when I barely want to cook and serve it with tostadas, avocados, and hot sauce. Just mix, marinate, and eat—instantly refreshing.

2 pounds imitation crab, shredded (see Tip)

4 ripe Roma (plum) tomatoes, diced

2 cucumbers, diced

1 cup roughly chopped fresh cilantro

½ red onion, diced (about ½ cup)

3 fresh chiles, seeded and finely chopped

1½ cups Clamato juice

1 cup fresh lime juice (about 6 to 8 limes)

Salt and ground black pepper

For Serving:
Tostadas
Sliced avocado
Hot sauce

In a large bowl, stir together the imitation crab, tomatoes, cucumbers, cilantro, onion, and jalapeños until combined.

In a large measuring cup, whisk together the Clamato and lime juice. Pour the mixture into the bowl with the crab, season with a pinch each of salt and black pepper, and mix until evenly combined. Cover with a lid or plastic wrap and place in the refrigerator to marinate and chill for 2 to 4 hours.

Evenly divide the chilled salad among six bowls and serve with tostadas, avocado, and hot sauce.

COCINA TIP:

- I like to use my stand mixer with the paddle attachment to shred the crab.

DAD'S SHRIMP COCKTAIL

Serves 8

Total time: 15 minutes, plus 2 to 4 hours marinating time

American shrimp cocktail and Mexican shrimp cocktail are more like cousins than twins, and if you haven't had the Mexican variety, you're missing something. This is my dad's recipe, and it hits all the right notes—spicy, salty, and herbaceous. He mixes Clamato juice with ketchup, a few cucumbers, cilantro, and hot sauce. We always use saltines to scoop up the tender shrimp and spicy sauce; you can also try it with tostadas. Let the flavors marinate for a couple of hours before digging in.

½ white onion, peeled

4 garlic cloves, peeled but whole

1 bay leaf

1 tablespoon salt

3 pounds jumbo shrimp, peeled and deveined (see Tip)

4 ripe Roma (plum) tomatoes, roughly chopped

2 large cucumbers, roughly chopped

2 cups Clamato juice

1½ cups ketchup

1 cup finely chopped fresh cilantro

Juice of 3 limes

Salt and ground black pepper

For Serving:
Saltines or tostadas

Thinly sliced avocado

Hot sauce

Prepare an ice bath by filling a large bowl halfway with ice and cold water; have it near the stove. Fill a large pot with water and add the onion, garlic, bay leaf, and salt. Bring to a boil over medium heat. Add the shrimp and cook until pink and opaque, about 7 minutes. Using a slotted spoon or fine-mesh sieve, transfer the shrimp to the prepared ice bath to stop the cooking. Let cool for at least 5 minutes, then drain the shrimp and transfer to a large bowl. Discard the onion, garlic, and bay leaf.

Add the tomatoes, cucumbers, Clamato, ketchup, cilantro, lime juice, and a pinch each of salt and black pepper to the bowl with the shrimp. Mix to evenly combine. Cover with plastic wrap and place in the refrigerator to marinate and chill for 2 to 4 hours.

Evenly divide the chilled mixture among eight bowls. Serve with saltines or tostadas, sliced avocado, and hot sauce.

COCINA TIP:

- I highly recommend buying peeled and deveined shrimp. It may cost a little more, but doing it yourself will add 45 minutes. Trust me, it takes about 40 seconds to do one shrimp—I timed it!

TUNA SALAD

Serves 4

Total time: 15 minutes, plus 1 hour marinating time

Basic tuna salad just won't cut it when my little brothers come over. This light and bright dish is brimming with fantastic flavors—sweet corn, the heat of fresh jalapeños, the brine of pickled jalapeños, and the crunch of red and green bell peppers. I like spiking the mayo dressing with yellow mustard and serving it over chopped avocado with saltines. Serve this for family lunch or a picnic, and I promise it'll change your mind about what a tuna salad can be!

4 (5-ounce) cans water-packed tuna, drained

3 ripe Roma (plum) tomatoes, diced

1 cup thinly shredded romaine lettuce

1 green bell pepper, finely chopped

1 red bell pepper, finely chopped

½ red onion, diced (about ½ cup)

¼ cup finely chopped fresh cilantro

1 (4-ounce) can corn kernels, drained

2 fresh jalapeño chiles, finely diced, plus more for garnish

1 cup mayonnaise

⅓ cup brine from a jar of pickled jalapeños

2 tablespoons yellow mustard

Juice of ½ lime

Salt and ground black pepper

For Serving:
Pickled jalapeños
Diced avocado
Saltines

In a large bowl, combine the tuna, tomatoes, lettuce, bell peppers, onion, cilantro, corn, and diced jalapeños and mix until evenly combined.

In a medium bowl, whisk together the mayonnaise, jalapeño brine, mustard, and lime juice. Season with a big pinch each of salt and black pepper.

Pour the mayonnaise mixture into the bowl with the tuna and use a spatula or a spoon to mix until combined. Taste and season with more salt and black pepper, if needed. Refrigerate, uncovered, for 1 hour to allow the flavors to marinate and chill.

Evenly divide the chilled salad among four bowls and serve with pickled jalapeños, avocado, and saltines.

COCINA TIP:

- You can make this salad a day in advance. Refrigerate in a sealed container until ready to serve. Just leave out the romaine and cilantro, then add them about 1 hour before serving.

CHICKEN WITH ALFREDO PASTA

Serves 6

Total time: 1 hour

I used to order this every time we went to an Italian restaurant because I thought it was too complicated to make at home. I ordered it enough times and asked enough questions to finally figure it out, and with time and practice, my version got to be just as good! It's a simple dish that tastes pretty fancy, and I hope you'll make it for your family. My daughter loves this with steamed broccoli and a slice of lemon.

2 teaspoons salt, plus a big pinch

1 pound linguine

3 boneless, skinless chicken breasts

2 teaspoons dried basil

2 teaspoons chili powder

2 teaspoons garlic powder

2 teaspoons onion powder

2 teaspoons dried oregano

1 teaspoon ground black pepper

6 tablespoons (¾ stick) unsalted butter

2 tablespoons extra-virgin olive oil

5 garlic cloves, minced

¼ cup all-purpose flour

1½ cups heavy cream

8 ounces cream cheese, at room temperature

1 cup freshly grated Parmesan cheese

Juice of 1 lemon

Finely chopped fresh parsley, for garnish

Lemon wedges, for serving

Fill a large pot of water, add a big pinch of salt, and bring to a boil over high heat. Add the pasta and cook, stirring occasionally, until al dente according to the package directions. Reserve 1 cup of the pasta cooking water, and drain.

Meanwhile, place the chicken between two layers of parchment paper on a cutting board. Using a meat mallet or the bottom of a small saucepan, pound the meat until it is about ¼ inch thick.

In a small bowl, whisk together the basil, chili powder, garlic powder, onion powder, oregano, salt, and black pepper. Set aside 1½ tablespoons of the seasoning mix. Sprinkle the remaining seasoning mix over the chicken to evenly coat.

Heat 3 tablespoons of the butter and the oil in a large cast-iron skillet over medium heat. Add the chicken to the pan and cook until golden brown on both sides, about 6 minutes per side. Transfer to a plate to rest for 5 minutes. Thinly slice each breast lengthwise, across the grain into 1-inch wide strips.

In the same skillet, melt the remaining 3 tablespoons butter over medium heat. Add the garlic and cook, stirring constantly, until fragrant, about 1 minute. Be careful not to let it burn. Stir in the reserved 1½ tablespoons seasoning mix and the flour and cook, stirring constantly, until lightly toasted and fragrant, 30 seconds to 1 minute. Pour in the heavy cream and stir to evenly combine. Add the reserved 1 cup pasta cooking water, the cream cheese, Parmesan, and lemon juice and mix well. Bring to a simmer over medium to medium-low heat and cook, stirring occasionally, for 5 minutes to meld the flavors.

Add the cooked pasta to the pan and use tongs to gently combine the pasta and sauce.

Evenly divide the pasta among six pasta bowls. Top with the sliced chicken. Garnish with parsley and lemon wedges for squeezing.

MY MOM'S HAM AND CHEESE SPAGHETTI

Serves 4

Total time: 25 minutes

This is the one standout recipe that reminds me of every generation in my family, from Abuela Amelia to my mother, Lorena, and now me, Izzy's mom! My husband and daughter are superfans, too, and I'm so proud to carry on the tradition. The noodles are bathed in the creamiest, cheesiest sauce studded with sweet nuggets of ham. My brothers are also crazy about it and expect an enormous bowl to be ready for them every time they come over. It's an ideal quick pantry meal, and is even better with the Milanesa de Res (page 107) or anything fried. A dollop of crema Mexicana adds richness and a little tang.

Salt

1 pound spaghetti

1 tablespoon unsalted butter

¼ white onion, peeled and diced (about ¼ cup)

2 garlic cloves, minced

10 thick slices deli ham (see Tips), diced

1½ cups crema Mexicana (see Tips)

1 cup shredded mozzarella cheese

1½ teaspoons chicken bouillon powder, preferably Knorr

Ground black pepper

Finely chopped fresh curly parsley, for garnish

Bring a large pot of water to a boil over high heat with a big pinch of salt. Add the spaghetti and cook, stirring occasionally, until al dente according to the package directions. Drain and transfer to a serving bowl.

Meanwhile, melt the butter in a large nonstick skillet over medium heat. Add the onion and garlic and cook, stirring occasionally, until the onion is translucent, 5 to 7 minutes. Add the ham and cook, stirring, for about 3 minutes to warm the ham through. Stir in the crema, mozzarella, and bouillon powder and bring to a simmer, and cook, stirring occasionally, until slightly thickened, about 4 minutes. Season with a pinch each of salt and pepper.

Pour the sauce into the bowl with the cooked spaghetti and stir to evenly coat the noodles. Taste and adjust the seasoning as needed.

Evenly divide the pasta among four pasta bowls. Garnish with a sprinkle of parsley and serve.

COCINA TIPS:

- I like the bite of white onion, but yellow is a fine substitute.

- If you can, ask the deli counter to slice the ham a little thicker, about ¼ inch thick. Otherwise, the ham slices stick together when you dice them and won't be as evenly distributed.

- If you can't find crema Mexicana, use the same amount of sour cream thinned with a little milk.

- On the rare chance there are leftovers, I like to stir in a little more crema or 2% milk and reheat them in the microwave.

BRANDON'S SHRIMP PASTA

Serves 4 to 6

Total time: 30 minutes

A Mex-Italian mash-up you didn't know you needed! Chipotle powder and chipotles in adobo are blended with cream cheese, crema Mexicana, and seasoning and then tossed with sweet shrimp and spaghetti for an unforgettable spicy seafood pasta dinner. Izzy always sprinkles the hot dish with a big handful of cheese the minute I set it down, so it's extra gooey and cheesy.

1½ pounds large shrimp, peeled and deveined

⅓ cup canola or other neutral oil, plus more as needed

1 teaspoon chipotle powder

½ teaspoon garlic powder

½ teaspoon onion powder

1 tablespoon plus ½ teaspoon salt

½ teaspoon ground black pepper

1 pound spaghetti

2 bay leaves

3 ripe Roma (plum) tomatoes, quartered

¼ small white onion, peeled and sliced (about ¼ cup)

3 garlic cloves, peeled but whole

2 chipotle peppers from canned chipotles in adobo sauce, or more for added spice

4 ounces cream cheese, at room temperature

½ cup crema Mexicana (see Tip)

1 tablespoon adobo seasoning

1 tablespoon chicken bouillon powder, preferably Knorr

Freshly grated Parmesan cheese, for garnish (optional)

In a large bowl, combine the shrimp, oil, chipotle powder, garlic powder, onion powder, ½ teaspoon of the salt, and a pinch of black pepper and mix well until coated.

Heat a large skillet over medium heat. Add the shrimp in a single layer, making sure not to overcrowd the pan, and cook until they turn pink and opaque on the bottom, about 3 minutes. Flip and cook until opaque on the other side, about 2 minutes more. Transfer to a plate to cool. Reserve the skillet.

Bring a large pot of water to a boil over high heat. Add the pasta, bay leaves, and remaining 1 tablespoon salt and cook, stirring occasionally, until al dente according to the package directions. Drain the pasta, discard the bay leaves, and set aside.

Return the skillet used for the shrimp to medium heat, adding more oil if the pan seems dry. Add the tomatoes, onion, and garlic and cook, stirring occasionally, until the onion is softened and translucent, about 3 minutes. Transfer to a blender along with the chipotles, cream cheese, crema, adobo seasoning, and bouillon powder and blend on high until smooth.

Drizzle some oil into the skillet and heat over medium-low heat. Add the sauce and bring to a simmer, then cook, stirring occasionally, until warmed through and thickened, about 10 minutes. Add the pasta and shrimp and toss until combined.

Divide the pasta evenly among bowls and garnish with Parmesan, if desired.

COCINA TIP:

- If you can't find crema Mexicana, thin the same amount of sour cream with a little milk.

SPAGHETTI WITH POBLANO CHILE SAUCE

Serves 4 or 5 *Total time: 35 minutes*

Mexican pasta probably isn't something you've thought about before, but this poblano sauce may have you rethinking your devotion to the red variety. Slightly sweet with a bit of heat, roasted poblanos are blitzed with cream cheese, sour cream, and, if you can take the heat, some fresh jalapeños. This is one of Izzy's favorite recipes, and I love to remind her that even if it's a little too spicy, we must endure it, because we're Mexican and love our spicy food! It's fancy enough to serve to company and delight vegetarians (see Tips). Sometimes we go all out and have it alongside our Milanesa de Res (page 107).

4 fresh poblano chiles

2 bay leaves

1 small white onion, halved and peeled

1 tablespoon salt, plus more as needed

1 pound spaghetti

2 tablespoons canola or other neutral oil

1 cup crema Mexicana (see Tips)

4 ounces cream cheese, at room temperature

Leaves and 2-inch stems from 1 small cilantro

2 fresh jalapeños, optional

2 garlic cloves, peeled but whole

1 tablespoon chicken bouillon powder, preferably Knorr

Ground black pepper

Crumbled queso fresco, for serving

Finely chopped fresh cilantro, for garnish

Heat a large skillet over medium heat. Add the poblanos and turn them with tongs so they char on every side, about 5 minutes per side. (Alternatively, place them on a baking sheet and broil until the skins start to blacken, about 5 minutes per side.) Wipe the skillet clean and set aside. Transfer the chiles to a large bowl, cover with a kitchen towel, and let steam for 5 minutes. Carefully remove the chiles from the bowl and set aside until cool enough to handle, then peel them and discard the skin, stems, and seeds.

Meanwhile, fill a large pot with water and add the bay leaves, ½ onion, and the salt. Bring to a boil over medium heat. Stir in the spaghetti and cook, stirring occasionally, until al dente according to the package directions. Reserve ½ cup of the pasta cooking water, then drain the spaghetti and discard the bay leaves and onion. Return the spaghetti to the pot, add 1 tablespoon of the oil, and toss to evenly coat the noodles. Cover lightly with aluminum foil and set aside.

In a blender, combine the roasted poblanos, reserved pasta water, remaining ½ onion, the crema, cream cheese, cilantro, jalapeños (if using), garlic, bouillon powder, and a big pinch each of salt and black pepper. Blend on high until smooth, about 45 seconds. Taste and adjust the seasoning as desired.

RECIPE CONTINUES

Heat the remaining 1 tablespoon oil in the same skillet over medium heat. Pour the sauce into the pan and bring to a simmer, then cook, stirring occasionally, until thickened, about 10 minutes.

Stir the pasta into the sauce and cook until warm and creamy, about 2 minutes.

Divide the pasta evenly among bowls. Sprinkle with queso fresco, and garnish with fresh cilantro, and serve.

COCINA TIPS:

- To make this completely vegetarian, use veggie bouillon in place of the chicken.

- If you can't find crema Mexicana, thin the same amount of sour cream with a little milk.

TACOS DE PAPA

Serves 4 to 6   *Total time: 1 hour 15 minutes*

This was one of my mom's greatest hits for a weeknight dinner; she'd plan and boil some potatoes the day before so everything could be easily mixed and tossed into a tortilla. Like my mom, I make this family favorite on a busy weeknight, and I'm so glad I get to share it with you. The filling is smooth mashed potatoes with cooked tomato salsa and just enough mozzarella to play off the fried tortillas' crispiness and ooze when you bite into it. Cheese Pull Alert!! Topped with crema Mexicana, refreshing shredded iceberg, and red onions, these are always part of our Super Bowl snack spread.

5 russet potatoes, peeled and cut into large chunks

2½ teaspoons salt, plus more if needed

1 cup canola or other neutral oil, plus more as needed

½ small white onion, chopped (about ⅓ cup)

3 garlic cloves, minced

4 ripe Roma (plum) tomatoes, chopped

2 fresh jalapeños, seeded and finely chopped

1 teaspoon dried oregano

1½ cups shredded mozzarella cheese

½ teaspoon ground black pepper

20 corn tortillas

For Serving:
Crema Mexicana (see Tips)
Shredded iceberg lettuce
Thinly sliced red onions
Crumbled queso fresco
Salsa Roja (page 225) or store-bought salsa

Place the potatoes in a large pot and add 2 teaspoons of the salt and enough water to just cover them. Cover and bring to a boil over medium heat. Uncover, reduce the heat to medium-low, and simmer until the potatoes are fork-tender, about 45 minutes. Drain the potatoes and transfer to a large bowl. Use a potato masher or ricer to mash until they are very smooth. Set aside.

Heat ½ cup of the oil in a large skillet over medium heat. Add the onion and garlic and cook, stirring occasionally, until translucent and fragrant, about 7 minutes. Stir in the tomatoes, jalapeños, and oregano and cook, stirring occasionally, until softened, about 3 minutes.

Transfer the vegetable mixture to the bowl with the mashed potatoes and add the mozzarella, remaining ½ teaspoon salt, and the black pepper. Using a silicone spatula or wooden spoon, mix to evenly combine. Taste and add more salt if needed. Wipe the pan clean and set aside.

Wrap half the tortillas in damp paper towels and microwave until they can fold without cracking, 30 seconds to 1 minute. Repeat with the remaining tortillas.

Place the tortillas on a large baking sheet or directly on your countertop. Spread the potato filling over one half of each tortilla, dividing it evenly among them. Fold the tortillas in half over the filling, pressing to seal.

RECIPE CONTINUES

Set a wire rack over a baking sheet and have it near the stove. In the skillet you used for the vegetables, heat the remaining ½ cup oil over medium heat. Working in batches to avoid crowding the pan, add the folded tortillas to the pan and fry until golden brown and crispy, using tongs or a slotted spoon to flip them halfway, 2 to 3 minutes per side. Transfer the tortillas to the wire rack to drain and repeat with the remaining tortillas, adding more oil between batches if needed.

Divide the tacos among plates. Drizzle with crema and top with lettuce, onion, queso fresco, and salsa and serve.

COCINA TIPS:

- This recipe can come together in only 30 minutes if you have leftover mashed potatoes on hand. (The leftover potato mixture from Edith's Chiles Rellenos, page 123, can be used for this recipe.) Or just plan ahead and parboil the potatoes the night before. Drain and store in an airtight container in the refrigerator for up to 2 days.

- Don't let the tacos sit too long after filling and folding, as the tortillas will start to dry out and crack along the seam. You can keep them covered with a moist paper towel to help prevent this.

- If you can't find crema Mexicana, thin the same amount of sour cream with a little milk.

TACOS DE CAMARONES

Serves 6

Total time: 30 minutes, plus 1 hour refrigeration time

A perfect pairing: batter-fried shrimp and cool creamy coleslaw! Making these takes me back to those sweet beach vacations with my family, crunching away at plates of seaside fresh shrimp tacos after a long day under the sun. Yellow mustard is my surprise ingredient in the batter because I love the way it rounds out the bite of the chili powder and spices. Make the coleslaw about an hour before you cook the shrimp so its flavors can come together.

Coleslaw:

3 cups thinly shredded red cabbage

3 medium carrots, peeled and coarsely grated

½ cup mayonnaise

¼ cup sour cream

¼ cup finely chopped fresh cilantro

Juice of 1 large lime

1 teaspoon granulated sugar

½ teaspoon salt, plus more as needed

½ teaspoon ground black pepper, plus more as needed

Make the coleslaw:

In a large bowl, combine the cabbage, carrots, mayonnaise, sour cream, cilantro, lime juice, sugar, salt, and black pepper and mix well. Taste and adjust the seasoning as desired. Cover with plastic wrap and refrigerate while you cook the shrimp.

Cook the shrimp:

In a large bowl, toss the shrimp with ½ teaspoon each of the salt and black pepper.

In another large bowl, whisk together the flour, chili powder, garlic powder, oregano, and remaining ½ teaspoon each salt and black pepper. Slowly whisk in the eggs and mustard until evenly combined. Whisk in the beer (or sparkling water, if using) until the batter is smooth and no lumps remain. It should have the consistency of pancake batter and coat the shrimp easily, so add a splash more beer if needed to achieve that.

Shrimp:

Shrimp:

2 pounds jumbo shrimp, peeled and deveined

1 teaspoon salt

1 teaspoon ground black pepper

2 cups all-purpose flour

½ teaspoon chili powder

½ teaspoon garlic powder

½ teaspoon dried oregano

2 large eggs, beaten

2 teaspoons yellow mustard

8 ounces beer or sparkling water, plus more as needed

2 cups canola or other neutral oil, for frying

18 corn tortillas

Chipotle Salsa (page 227), for serving

Set a wire rack over a baking sheet and have it near the stove. Heat the oil in a large skillet over medium heat. To check that the oil is hot enough for frying, dip a toothpick in the oil; if the oil bubbles, it's ready. Working in batches to avoid crowding the pan, dip the shrimp into the batter one at a time and carefully place them in the hot oil. Cook, turning once, until golden brown, and cooked through, about 3 minutes. Using a slotted spoon or tongs, transfer the shrimp to the wire rack to cool slightly and repeat with the remaining shrimp.

To assemble:

Heat a comal, griddle, or dry skillet over medium heat. Working in batches, heat the tortillas for 45 seconds per side and transfer to a plate.

Place 3 tortillas on each plate. Spoon ¼ cup of the coleslaw onto each tortilla and top with 2 or 3 shrimp. Drizzle with chipotle salsa and serve.

COCINA TIP:

- For a quick slaw, buy a 14-ounce bag of coleslaw mix in place of the cabbage and carrots.

ENCHILADAS ROJAS

Serves 4

Total time: 1 hour

These enchiladas remind me of my childhood dinners. Spicy and cheesy, with a bit of bite from the raw onion, these authentic enchiladas are nothing like the bland versions you may be familiar with. While the sauce takes about 20 minutes, you can make a big batch over the weekend so it's available for a quick weeknight dinner (see Tip). I serve this with a side of pan-seared diced potatoes and carrots, but any veg will do. The enchiladas are so simple that your family will fall in love with this recipe, just like I did, eating them at my family parties in Mexico.

For the enchilada sauce:
7 dried guajillo chiles, stemmed, split, and seeded
4 dried chiles de árbol, whole
2 dried ancho chiles, stemmed, split, and seeded
½ white onion peeled and roughly chopped (about ½ cup)
3 garlic cloves, peeled but whole
½ tablespoon chicken bouillon powder, preferably Knorr
¼ teaspoon ground cumin
¼ teaspoon dried oregano

For the Enchiladas:
Canola or other neutral oil, as needed
12 corn tortillas
2 cups crumbled queso fresco
1 cup finely chopped white onion

For Serving:
Shredded lettuce
Roma (plum) tomatoes, sliced into half-moons
Sour cream

In a large pot, combine the guajillo chiles, chiles de árbol, ancho chiles, and enough water to just cover. Bring to a boil over high heat and lower the heat to medium and simmer until the skins soften, about 5 minutes.

Use a slotted spoon to transfer the softened chiles to a blender. Add the onion, garlic, bouillon powder, cumin, oregano, a pinch each of salt and black pepper and 1 cup water. With the steam vent in the blender top open, blend on high until smooth, with the texture resembling tomato sauce, about 45 seconds. If too thick, add up to ½ cup more water and blend until smooth, about 20 seconds.

Transfer the sauce to a large skillet set over medium heat. Bring the sauce to a simmer and cook, stirring frequently, until thickened, about 10 minutes.

Set a wire rack over a baking sheet and have it near the stove.

Heat 1 tablespoon of oil in a large skillet or comal over medium heat. Working with one at a time, dip a tortilla into the sauce, carefully place it in the skillet, and cook until it sizzles, about 5 seconds per side. Transfer the tortillas to the wire rack and repeat with the remaining tortillas, adding more oil as needed.

Sprinkle 2 generous tablespoons of queso fresco in the center of each tortilla and top with a heaping tablespoon of the onion. Tightly roll up the filled tortilla into a cigar shape.

Divide the enchiladas among four plates. Top with extra sauce, lettuce, tomatoes, and sour cream and serve.

COCINA TIP:
- The sauce can be made ahead and refrigerated in a sealed container for up to 5 days or freeze for up to 2 months.

ENCHILADAS VERDES

Serves 4

Total time: 1 hour 15 minutes

There are so many enchilada varieties, but if forced to pick my favorite, I'd have to say the green ones—enchiladas verdes. They are mellow and tangy, savory and delicious, and the spices are just right. I remember coming home from school to the smell of tortillas frying, and I knew my mom was making my favorite enchiladas. She still loves making them for us to this day, even though we are all adults now!

Chicken:

2 pounds bone-in, skinless chicken breasts

½ small white onion, peeled

1 head garlic, halved horizontally

3 bay leaves

1 tablespoon salt

1 tablespoon ground black pepper

Sauce:

8 fresh serrano chiles or jalapeños

2 pounds tomatillos, husked and rinsed (see Tips)

½ small white onion, peeled

4 garlic cloves, peeled but whole

Leaves and 2-inch stems from 1 small cilantro

1 tablespoon salt

2 tablespoons canola or other neutral oil

Cook the chicken:

In 4-quart pot, combine the chicken, onion, garlic, bay leaves, salt, black pepper, and 8 cups water (or enough to cover the chicken) and bring to a boil over medium heat. Cook until the chicken is tender, about 30 minutes, occasionally skimming and discarding any white foam from the surface of the water.

Remove the chicken from the broth with tongs and transfer to a large plate. When it's cool enough to handle, pull the meat off the bones; discard the bones and shred the meat with two forks or your hands. Strain the broth through a fine-mesh sieve into a large heatproof bowl. Discard the onion, garlic, and bay leaves. Set aside 1 cup of the broth to use in the sauce and transfer the remainder to an airtight container and save it for another use (see Tips).

Make the sauce:

Bring a medium pot of water to a boil over medium heat. Add the chiles and maintain a simmer for 4 minutes. Remove the pot from the heat and add the tomatillos. Let stand until the color of the tomatillos changes to a lighter green, 30 seconds to 1 minute. Drain the chiles and tomatillos and set aside to cool slightly. Wipe the pot dry and set aside.

Transfer the cooled chiles and tomatillos to a blender and add the onion, garlic, cilantro, salt, and reserved 1 cup broth. With the steam vent in the blender top open, blend until smooth, about 1 minute.

Heat the oil in the reserved pot over medium heat. Add the sauce and bring to a simmer, stir, and remove from heat. Season with salt to taste.

INGREDIENTS CONTINUE

RECIPE CONTINUES

Enchiladas:

2 tablespoons canola or other neutral oil, or more as needed

12 corn tortillas

For Serving:

Shredded iceberg lettuce

Diced Roma (plum) tomatoes

Diced red onion

Pickled jalapeños

Sour cream

Crumbled queso fresco

Make the enchiladas:

Have a large serving platter and a plate near the stove. Heat the oil in a large skillet over medium heat. Use tongs to dip each tortilla, one at a time, into the sauce, then place the tortilla in the hot skillet and cook until soft on both sides, about 5 seconds per side and transfer to a plate to fill. (I fill one enchilada at a time. If you prefer to cook all of the tortillas before filling them, make sure to keep them wrapped in a kitchen towel to stay warm.)

Place 2 tablespoons of the shredded chicken on each tortilla and roll it up tightly, placing them on a large platter as you go. Top with the remaining sauce.

Place 3 enchiladas on each plate. Top with lettuce, tomatoes, onion, pickled jalapeños, sour cream, and queso fresco and enjoy!

COCINA TIPS:

- I prefer bone-in chicken as it adds more flavor and richness. If you can only find bone-in, skin-on chicken breasts, remove the skin before cooking. This makes the broth less oily.

- Remove the seeds from the chiles before blending if you prefer less heat.

- To clean tomatillos, first remove the outer husk, then thoroughly clean with cool water and fruit and veggie wash or natural dish soap to remove the sticky residue.

- If you're not using the broth immediately, refrigerate in a sealed container for up to 3 days or in the freezer for up to 3 months.

FRIED QUESADILLAS

Serves 4 to 6
(makes 12 quesadillas)

Total time: 30 minutes

While I can't stop myself from ordering these in a restaurant, I also craved a version for home. A cheese-stuffed corn tortilla heated in a pan is probably the easiest homemade snack in history, but this gets an added boost with a few items you can have in your fridge already—either my homemade Chile de Árbol Salsa (page 228) or Salsa Verde (page 235), or store-bought salsa. Use store-bought tortillas or make my easy homemade corn tortillas (page 222), and try stuffing them with leftover Pollo Asado (page 54), chopped Carne Asada (page 108), or leftover veggies.

Filling:
3 tablespoons canola or other neutral oil

3 ripe Roma (plum) tomatoes, roughly chopped

½ white onion, peeled and diced (about ½ cup)

3 fresh jalapeños, minced

½ teaspoon salt

½ teaspoon ground black pepper

½ cup finely chopped fresh cilantro

Quesadillas:
12 corn tortillas

1 cup shredded queso Oaxaca or mozzarella cheese

½ cup canola or other neutral oil, for frying

Shredded cabbage, for garnish

Chile de Árbol Salsa (page 228) or Salsa Verde (page 235), for serving

Make the filling:
Heat the oil in a small saucepan over medium heat. Add the tomatoes, onion, jalapeños, salt, and black pepper and cook, stirring occasionally, until the onion is softened, about 7 minutes. Stir in the cilantro. Set aside.

Make the quesadillas:
Set a wire rack over a baking sheet and have it near the stove.

Place the tortillas on a work surface and top one half of each tortilla with cheese, dividing it evenly among them. Top the cheese with the filling. Gently fold the tortillas over the cheese and press the edges together tightly to seal.

Heat the oil in a large skillet over medium heat. To check that the oil is hot enough for frying, dip a wooden toothpick in the oil; if the oil bubbles, it's ready. Use a slotted spoon or tongs to carefully place 2 quesadillas in the oil and cook, undisturbed, until golden brown and crispy on the bottom, about 2 minutes. Use tongs or a slotted spoon to flip them and cook until golden brown and crispy on the second side, about 2 minutes more. Transfer to the wire rack to drain and repeat with the remaining quesadillas.

Transfer the quesadillas to a large serving platter. Sprinkle with cabbage and spoon salsa over the quesadillas, then serve.

CHICKEN MARSALA

Serves 2 to 4

Total time: 45 minutes

I learned this recipe from my mother-in-law, Verena, and I'm so glad we get to include one of her cherished traditions in our family. The trick is to add a splash of sweet-and-sour balsamic vinegar to the creamy mushroom sauce to deepen the flavor. It's so pretty with a sprinkle of chopped fresh parsley. Don't forget to serve with rice, mashed potatoes, or crusty bread to soak up that addictive sauce.

½ cup all-purpose flour

Salt

Ground black pepper

4 chicken cutlets, pounded thin

5 tablespoons unsalted butter

1 tablespoon extra-virgin olive oil

8 ounces baby bella (cremini) mushrooms, thinly sliced

3 garlic cloves, minced

1 shallot, minced

½ teaspoon smoked paprika

¾ cup Marsala wine

½ cup chicken broth

½ cup heavy cream

1 tablespoon balsamic vinegar

1 tablespoon finely chopped fresh parsley, for garnish

Spread the flour over a large plate. Season both sides of the chicken with salt and black pepper. Dredge the chicken in the flour to coat both sides and tap to remove excess flour.

Heat the butter and the olive oil in a large skillet over medium heat. Add the chicken in a single layer and sear until golden brown and fully cooked through, 4 to 6 minutes per side. Transfer to a plate and cover with foil to keep warm. Wipe the skillet clean.

In the same skillet, combine the mushrooms, garlic, shallot, paprika, and ½ teaspoon each of salt and black pepper. Cook, stirring occasionally, until the mushrooms are tender and golden brown, 3 to 5 minutes. Pour in the Marsala and broth and cook, stirring frequently, until the wine reduces slightly, about 4 minutes. Pour in the cream and cook, stirring occasionally, until thickened, about 4 minutes.

Stir in the vinegar and simmer until thickened, about 3 minutes.

Reduce the heat to low, return the cooked chicken to the pan, and cook for about 4 minutes to heat through, stirring midway through.

Divide evenly among plates. Garnish with the parsley and serve.

POLLO A LA CHIPOTLE

Serves 4 to 6

Total time: 20 minutes, plus marinating time

Why stop at Chipotle when you can make this chipotle chicken right at home? It *is* a Mexican ingredient, after all, and I can never get enough of these smoked fresh jalapeños in their deep red sauce. I prefer boneless chicken thighs for their tenderness and flavor, but you can use steak or pork. You'll need to remember to marinate the meat in the morning or the night before. Make a double batch of the chipotle sauce, because it's great to have on hand for bowls, burritos, and quesadillas.

Chipotle Sauce:

½ cup olive oil

½ cup finely chopped fresh cilantro

½ small white onion, peeled and finely chopped (about ¼ cup)

4 garlic cloves, minced

3 chipotle peppers from canned chipotles in adobo sauce, diced, plus 1 tablespoon adobo sauce

2 teaspoons chili powder

2 teaspoons salt

1 teaspoon ground black pepper

1 teaspoon dried oregano

½ teaspoon ground cumin

Chicken:

2 pounds boneless, skinless chicken thighs, cut into 1-inch pieces

¼ cup canola or other neutral oil

For Serving:

Arroz Blanco (page 164)

Frijoles de Edith (page 171), warmed, or store-bought refried beans

Edith's Favorite Guacamole (page 236) or store-bought

Make the chipotle sauce:
In a large bowl, combine the olive oil, cilantro, onion, garlic, chipotles, adobo sauce, chili powder, salt, black pepper, oregano, and cumin and mix until evenly combined.

Make the chicken:
Add the chicken to the sauce and mix well to coat. Cover the bowl with plastic wrap and refrigerate for at least 4 hours or overnight.

Heat the oil in a large skillet over medium heat. Add the chicken and the sauce and cook, stirring occasionally, until the chicken is cooked through, about 15 minutes.

Divide the chicken evenly among plates. Serve with rice, beans, and guacamole.

COCINA TIP:

- I don't suggest substituting chicken breasts for the thighs, as the dish will be too dry.

POLLO EN CHILE GUAJILLO

Serves 5

Total time: 1 hour 10 minutes

I have so many good memories of sitting at my abuela's table enjoying this pollo en chile guajillo recipe. It's very popular in Guanajuato, the region of central Mexico where my parents grew up. Guajillos bring low-to-medium heat, rich smokiness, a bit of fruitiness, and a vibrant red color to this dish, adding intense and satisfyingly complex flavor to everyday chicken.

Guajillo Sauce:

2 tablespoons canola or other neutral oil

8 dried guajillo chiles, stemmed, split, and seeded

3 ripe Roma (plum) tomatoes, quartered

½ medium white onion, peeled

5 garlic cloves, peeled but whole

1 tablespoon salt

1½ teaspoons dried oregano

Chicken:

2 tablespoons canola or other neutral oil

½ medium white onion, peeled and thinly sliced (about ½ cup)

1 bay leaf

10 chicken drumsticks, skin removed, or 3 pounds bone-in, skinless chicken thighs

Arroz Blanco (page 164), for serving

Make the guajillo sauce:

Heat 1 tablespoon of the oil in a large saucepan over medium-low heat. Add the chiles and cook, using a wooden spoon or spatula to move them around so that they do not burn, just until fragrant, about 1 minute. Transfer to a blender and set aside to cool.

Increase the heat under the saucepan to medium-high. Add the remaining 1 tablespoon oil, the tomatoes, onion, and garlic and cook, stirring occasionally, until the tomatoes are charred, about 5 minutes. Pour in 1 cup water, bring to a boil over high heat, and cook, stirring occasionally until the tomatoes are soft, about 5 minutes. Remove from the heat and let cool for about 10 minutes.

Carefully transfer the tomato mixture to the blender with the chiles. Wipe the pan clean and set aside. Add the salt, oregano, and ½ cup water to the blender. With the steam vent in the blender top open, blend until smooth, about 45 seconds. Strain the sauce through a fine-mesh sieve into a large measuring cup or bowl. You can use a spoon to help push the sauce through the sieve to extract as much of the liquid as possible from the solids. Discard the solids.

Cook the chicken:

In the pan you used for the tomato mixture, heat the oil over medium heat. Add the strained sauce, onion, bay leaf, and 2 cups water. Place the chicken directly in the sauce and bring to a boil. Reduce the heat to medium-low and cook, stirring occasionally, until the chicken is tender and falling off the bone, about 45 minutes. Discard the bay leaf.

Divide the chicken and sauce evenly among five bowls and serve with rice.

POZOLE VERDE

Serves 6 to 8

Total time: 1 hour 45 minutes

This Mexican green pozole is a lighter twist on the traditional pozole rojo, made with pork and red sauce. I love the freshness of this dish, which comes from simmering the chicken in salsa verde. Plus, unlike its rojo cousin, this recipe doesn't take all day to cook—it's ready in under 2 hours.

Chicken Broth:

4 pounds bone-in, skin-on chicken drumsticks and thighs

½ white onion, peeled

1 head garlic, top one-third sliced off to expose the cloves

4 bay leaves

1 tablespoon chicken bouillon, preferably Knorr

1 tablespoon salt, plus more as needed

1 (15-ounce) can hominy, drained

Green Sauce:

3 tablespoons canola or other neutral oil

15 tomatillos, husked, rinsed, and halved (see Tip)

3 fresh poblano chiles, stemmed, seeded, and roughly chopped

1 fresh Anaheim chile, stemmed, seeded, and roughly chopped

½ white onion, peeled and roughly chopped (about ¼ cup)

5 garlic cloves, peeled but whole

2 cups roughly chopped fresh cilantro

2 teaspoons dried oregano

1 teaspoon whole black peppercorns

For Serving:

Shredded green cabbage

Finely chopped fresh cilantro

Finely diced onion

Lime wedges

Make the chicken broth:

In a large pot, bring 3 quarts (12 cups) water to a boil over high heat. Add the chicken, onion, garlic, bay leaves, bouillon powder, and salt. Add more water if needed to cover the chicken. Bring the water back to a boil, then reduce the heat to maintain a simmer and cook until foam forms on the surface, about 5 minutes. Skim off the foam and simmer for 20 minutes, continuing to skim any foam as needed. Remove the chicken from the pot and allow it to cool slightly. Discard the skin, shred the meat, and set aside.

Add the hominy to the pot and cook, skimming occasionally, for 40 minutes. Remove and discard the onion, garlic, and bay leaves and return the shredded chicken to the pot.

Make the green sauce:

Heat the oil in a large skillet over medium heat. Add the tomatillos, poblanos, Anaheim, onion, and garlic and cook, stirring occasionally, until the tomatillos lighten in color and soften, about 10 minutes. Remove from the heat.

Transfer the tomatillo mixture to a blender and add the cilantro, oregano, peppercorns, and 1 cup of the broth from the pot with the chicken. With the steam vent open, blend until smooth, about 15 seconds.

Return the sauce to the pot with the chicken and hominy and cook over medium heat, stirring occasionally, for 30 minutes to meld the flavors. Taste and season with more salt.

Divide the pozole evenly among bowls and top each bowl with cabbage, cilantro, and onion. Serve with lime wedges for squeezing.

COCINA TIP:

- To clean tomatillos, first remove the outer husk, then thoroughly clean with cool water and fruit and veggie wash or natural dish soap to remove the sticky residue.

BEEF OR CHICKEN CUTLETS

Serves 6

Total time: 30 minutes, plus 1 hour refrigeration time

I can't get enough of anything crispy, and this recipe delivers crunch with every juicy bite. My mom always taught me to make extra because they make wonderful leftovers for lunch and snacking, but I have to hide the extra cutlets in the back of the fridge or someone will devour them all before I've had the chance! Heavy cream and Spanish smoked paprika add a rich smokiness that we hit with a squeeze of lime and a dash of hot sauce. I have yet to meet any kid (or adult) who doesn't love eating a fried cutlet.

2 pounds milanesa de res (see Tip), cut into 6 equal portions, or 6 boneless, skinless chicken breasts

2 large eggs

1 tablespoon heavy cream

1 teaspoon garlic powder

1 teaspoon onion powder

1 teaspoon smoked paprika

½ teaspoon salt

½ teaspoon ground black pepper

3 cups plain dried bread crumbs or panko bread crumbs

1 cup canola or other neutral oil

Spaghetti Verde (page 80; optional)

Place the beef between two layers of parchment paper on a cutting board. Using a meat pounder or the bottom of a small saucepan, pound the meat until it is about ¼ inch thick. Transfer to a large baking dish or container.

In a large bowl, whisk together the eggs, cream, garlic powder, onion powder, paprika, salt, and pepper. Pour the mixture over the beef and use tongs or your hands to thoroughly coat the meat. Cover with a lid or plastic wrap and refrigerate for at least 1 hour.

Place the bread crumbs in a large baking dish. Working with one piece at a time, press the meat into the crumbs to evenly coat both sides and place on a baking sheet or platter. Repeat with the remaining meat.

Set a wire rack over another baking sheet and have it near the stove. Heat the oil in a large skillet over medium heat. Working in batches to avoid crowding the pan, place the breaded meat into the pan and cook until golden brown, about 3 minutes per side. Using a slotted spoon or tongs, transfer to the wire rack to drain and repeat with the remaining meat.

Divide the meat evenly among six plates. Serve with pasta, if desired.

COCINA TIP:

- Milanesa de res is known by a few names, including flap meat, flap steak, bavette, and bottom sirloin flap.

CARNE ASADA

Serves 4 to 6

Total time: 30 minutes, plus 3 hours marinating time

This is an excellent meal on its own, in a taco, in a bowl, or, even more impressive, piled onto a plate of my Loaded Carne Asada Nachos (page 153). The authentic marinade is key: a combo of lime juice, orange juice, onions, garlic, and a blend of herbs and spices that tenderizes and flavors the beef. Just don't skimp on time. You'll need to let this marinate for at least 3 hours, preferably overnight, but the wait will be worth it. Of course, you can cook this steak on the stovetop, but if you have a grill, the extra bit of char you get *es stupendo!*

Juice of 2 oranges

Juice of 5 limes

½ white onion, peeled and thinly sliced (about ½ cup)

½ cup finely chopped fresh cilantro

¼ cup extra-virgin olive oil

4 garlic cloves, minced

2 fresh jalapeños, seeded and sliced into rings

1½ tablespoons salt

1 tablespoon ground black pepper

1½ teaspoons garlic powder

1½ teaspoons onion powder

1½ teaspoons paprika

3½ pounds carne ranchera (see Tips) or skirt steak

9 Mexican bulb onions (see Tips)

For Serving:

Arroz Rojo (page 167)

Frijoles de Edith (page 171), warmed, or store-bought refried beans

Edith's Favorite Guacamole (page 236) or store-bought

Warm corn tortillas

In a large bowl or large resealable plastic bag, combine the orange juice, lime juice, onion, cilantro, olive oil, garlic, jalapeños, salt, black pepper, garlic powder, onion powder, and paprika. Add the meat to the bowl or bag and use your hands to make sure the meat is fully coated in the marinade. Cover the bowl or seal the bag tightly and refrigerate for at least 3 hours.

Heat an outdoor grill to medium-high (or heat a grill pan over medium-high heat).

Remove the meat from the marinade, reserving the marinade and place it on the grill (or pan).

Place the Mexican onions alongside the beef. (If you are not grilling, cook the onions in the same pan used for the meat, see Tips.) Cook, basting the meat occasionally with the marinade, until the meat is mostly pink in the center with black char marks on the outside, 4 to 6 minutes on each side for medium. If you prefer well-done meat, cook it for 1 to 2 minutes more on each side. Transfer the grilled meat to a cutting board, cover with foil, and let rest for at least 5 minutes before slicing.

Slice the meat across the grain and arrange it on a large platter. Serve with rice, beans, guacamole, tortillas, and grilled bulb onions!

COCINA TIPS:

- Carne ranchera is known by a few names, including flap meat, flap steak, bavette, and bottom sirloin flap.

- Mexican bulb onions are like scallions, but larger.

- If you are cooking on the stovetop and the pan is too crowded, you can cook the bulb onions in the same pan while the meat is resting.

BISTEC A LA MEXICANA

Serves 4 to 6

Total time: 45 minutes

We don't eat steak often, but it's this recipe when we do. Tender beef strips are quickly cooked in a rich, chunky sauce made of tomatoes, white onions, and green chiles—all the Mexican flag colors. Serve with a big scoop of Mexican red rice and my pinto beans, plus a few of my homemade tortillas (corn or flour, it's up to you), and you have a restaurant-quality dish at home.

4 tablespoons canola or other neutral oil

4 ripe Roma (plum) tomatoes

1 white onion, peeled and halved

4 fresh serrano chiles

3 garlic cloves, peeled but whole

Salt

1 tablespoon chicken bouillon powder, preferably Knorr

2 pounds milanesa de res (see Tip), cut thinly sliced into strips

For Serving:

Arroz Rojo (page 167)

Frijoles de Edith (page 171), warmed, or store-bought refried beans

Warm corn or flour tortillas

Heat 1 tablespoon of the oil in a large skillet over medium-high heat. Add the tomatoes, ½ onion, serranos, and garlic and cook, stirring occasionally, until charred on all sides, about 10 minutes. Transfer the vegetables to a blender (or food processor) and add the bouillon, 1 cup water, and a pinch of salt. Pulse three to five times to create a chunky salsa. Wipe out the skillet, if needed.

Thinly slice the remaining onion half.

In the same skillet, heat the remaining 3 tablespoons oil over medium heat. Add the sliced onion and the beef strips and cook, stirring occasionally, until the juices have evaporated and the meat is golden brown, 15 to 20 minutes.

Pour the salsa into the pan and bring to a simmer, then reduce the heat to medium-low and simmer, stirring frequently, until the sauce has thickened, about 15 minutes.

Divide the beef mixture evenly among plates. Serve with rice, beans, and warm tortillas.

COCINA TIP:

- Milanesa de res is known by a few names, including flap meat, flap steak, bavette, and bottom sirloin flap.

MEXICAN CORN DOGS

Serves 4

Total time: 10 minutes, if using premade corn tortillas

Growing up, these corn dogs were my mom's go-to for an easy after-school snack. Kids adore them—ask my daughter, who still begs me to make them all the time. But here's the secret: Grown-ups like them just as much, because they're tasty and versatile, and there's no batter to fuss with. Just a quick roll in a tortilla and a pan-fry, and dinner is done!

8 corn tortillas

8 hot dogs

½ cup canola or other neutral oil

Ketchup, for serving

Mustard, for serving

Hot sauce (I prefer Tapatío), for serving

Wrap each tortilla in a paper towel and stack them on a microwave-safe plate. Microwave on high until the tortillas are warmed through, about 30 seconds.

Wrap each hot dog in a paper towel and place on a microwave-safe plate. Microwave on high until the hot dogs are warmed through, 40 to 50 seconds.

When the tortillas are cool enough to handle, lay them out on a clean work surface. Place a hot dog in the center of each tortilla and roll it up tightly. Stick a toothpick into the center of the hot dog to secure the tortilla in place.

Set a wire rack over a baking sheet and have it near the stove. Heat the oil in a large skillet over medium heat. Working in batches, if necessary, carefully place the wrapped hot dogs in the pan, seam-side down, and cook, flipping as needed, until golden brown on all sides, about 3 minutes total. Transfer to the wire rack to drain.

Arrange the corn dogs on a platter and serve with ketchup, mustard, and hot sauce.

COCINA TIP:

- Cut these into bite-size pieces for a fun party snack!

CENAS
FIN DE SEMANA

Tostadas de Tinga / *Spicy*
Shredded Chicken Tostadas

Quesabirria Tacos

Empanadas de Carne Molida

Edith's Chiles Rellenos

Flautas

Tostadas de Cueritos Estilo
Guanajuato / *Tostadas with Pork*

Rinds and Tomato Salsa

Sopes de Soy Chorizo

Gorditas de Pollo /
Stuffed Tortillas with Chicken

Costillas en Salsa /
Pork Ribs in Chile

Mississippi Pot Roast

Mole con Pollo

Caldo de Res /
Beef and Vegetable Soup

WEEKEND
DINNERS

SPICY SHREDDED CHICKEN TOSTADAS

Serves 6
(makes 12 tostadas)

Total time: 1 hour 20 minutes

This was one of the first dishes I made for my husband when we were newlyweds. I was inspired by a memory of my mom making these for my dad. My husband loved it immediately and still requests it, so much so that I'm sure he'd say it's his favorite Mexican dish.

1 white onion, peeled and halved

1 head garlic, top one-third sliced off to expose the cloves

3 bay leaves

1 tablespoon chicken bouillon powder, preferably Knorr

1 tablespoon salt

3 bone-in, skinless chicken breasts

7 ripe Roma (plum) tomatoes

3 chipotle peppers from chipotles in adobo sauce, plus 2 to 3 tablespoons adobo sauce from the can (optional)

2 tablespoons canola or other neutral oil

For Serving:

2 cups mashed Frijoles de Edith (page 171), warmed, or store-bought refried beans

12 tostadas

Shredded lettuce

Sour cream

Crumbled queso fresco

Salsa Verde (page 235; optional)

In a 5½-quart pot, combine 3 quarts water (12 cups), ½ onion, the garlic head, bay leaves, bouillon powder, and salt. Bring to a boil over high heat. Add the chicken, reduce the heat to medium-low, and simmer until the meat is tender, about 45 minutes. Transfer the chicken to a plate to cool.

Add the tomatoes to the pot and cook, stirring occasionally, until softened, about 12 minutes. Using a slotted spoon, transfer the tomatoes and onion half to a blender or food processor (reserve the liquid in the pot). Remove the head of garlic from the pot and carefully squeeze the cloves from the skins into the blender. Add the chipotles and adobo sauce (if using) to the blender, along with 1 cup of liquid from the pot (see Tips page 133, for what to do with the extra broth). With the steam vent in the blender top open, blend about 10 seconds. If the sauce seems too thick, add a bit more liquid from the pot.

Thinly slice the remaining ½ onion. Heat the oil in a large skillet over medium heat. Add the onion and cook, stirring frequently, until softened, about 2 minutes. Stir the sauce from the blender into the skillet. Reduce the heat to medium-low and simmer for 5 minutes to meld the flavors.

Meanwhile, use two forks or your fingers to shred the chicken (discard the bones). Add the chicken to the sauce and simmer, stirring occasionally, for about 10 minutes to allow the chicken to soak up the sauce. Discard the bay leaves.

To assemble:
Evenly spread the beans on the tostadas, spreading them to the edges. Top with the chicken, lettuce, sour cream, and queso fresco. Place 2 tostadas on each plate and drizzle with extra tinga sauce or salsa verde, if desired, and serve.

QUESABIRRIA TACOS

Serves 8

Total time: 45 minutes, plus 4 to 8 hours in a slow cooker or 3⅓ to 4 hours in the oven

Quesabirria is a delicious explosion of flavors and textures. Beef is braised in a seasoned chile-and-tomato sauce until it's tender and soft, then topped with cheese, nestled in a red-chile-sauce-soaked tortilla dripping with spice and flavor, and pan-fried for that irresistible crunch. It's traditionally served with a side of the reserved braising liquid, known as consommé, which is used as a dipping sauce to enhance the flavors with each bite. It's not a quick recipe, but it's certainly worth the effort.

Birria:

4 pounds chuck roast

Salt and ground black pepper

3 tablespoons canola or other neutral oil

8 to 10 dried guajillo chiles, stemmed, split, and seeded

2 dried pasilla chiles, stemmed, split, and seeded

5 dried chiles de árbol (or more if you prefer it spicier), stemmed, split, and seeded

3 dried puya chiles, stemmed, split, and seeded (see Tips; optional)

1 ripe Roma (plum) tomato

3 tablespoons distilled white vinegar

4 cups low-sodium beef broth

1 garlic clove, peeled but whole

3 whole cloves

1 teaspoon peeled and minced fresh ginger

1 teaspoon dried oregano

1 teaspoon whole black peppercorns

½ teaspoon ground cumin

2 bay leaves

Make the birria:

Pat the chuck roast dry and generously season on all sides with salt and black pepper. Heat the oil in a large skillet over medium-low heat. Carefully place the chuck roast into the pan and sear until golden brown on the bottom, about 3 minutes. Using tongs or a spatula, flip the meat and sear until golden brown on the other side, about 3 minutes more. Transfer the meat to a slow cooker.

In a large pot, combine 4 cups water, the guajillos, pasillas, chiles de árbol, puyas (if using), and tomato. Bring to a boil over high heat and cook until the chiles are softened, about 10 minutes. Using a slotted spoon, transfer the chiles and tomato to a blender and discard the water.

Add the vinegar, broth, garlic, cloves, ginger, oregano, peppercorns, and cumin to the blender. With the steam vent in the blender top open, blend on high until smooth, about 45 seconds. Strain the sauce through a fine-mesh sieve into the slow cooker with the meat, turning it to coat with the sauce. Add the bay leaves, cover, and cook on low for 4 to 8 hours, until the meat is tender and easy to shred with a fork. Transfer the meat to a large plate and set aside; discard the bay leaves.

Measure 2 cups of the sauce into a small pot and cover to keep warm (this is your consommé, which will be served alongside the tacos). Measure another 2 cups of the sauce into a wide bowl and set aside for dipping the tortillas.

Shred the meat, return it to the slow cooker, and mix it evenly with the remaining sauce.

Tacos:

2 tablespoons canola or other neutral oil, plus more as needed

8 corn tortillas

1 cup shredded queso Oaxaca or mozzarella cheese, plus more for garnish

For Serving:

Chopped white onion

Chopped fresh cilantro

Assemble the tacos:

Heat the oil in a medium skillet over low heat. Dip a tortilla into the reserved sauce to lightly coat, then place it in the hot skillet. Cook until softened, about 20 seconds per side, then top the tortilla with 2 tablespoons of the cheese and spoon some shredded beef on top. Fold the tortilla in half, like a quesadilla, and cook for 1 minute. Use tongs to flip the taco and cook until the cheese has melted, about 1 minute. Transfer the taco to a plate and repeat with the remaining tortillas, adding more oil to the skillet as needed.

Evenly divide the tacos among four plates. Garnish with onion, cilantro, cheese, and reserved sauce. Serve the reserved consommé in individual bowls alongside for dipping.

COCINA TIPS:

- Puya chiles have the same fruity flavor as guajillos, but are hotter. If you can't find them, the tacos will still be delicious!

- To make the birria in the oven: Stir the 3 tablespoons vinegar into 6 cups low-sodium beef broth instead of 4 cups. Add 2 cups of the vinegar-broth mixture to the blended sauce. Place the chuck roast, sauce, remaining 4 cups vinegar-broth mixture, and bay leaves in a large Dutch oven. Cover and cook in a 325°F oven for 3½ to 4 hours, stirring midway through, until the meat has softened. Remove 2 cups of sauce for the consommé and 2 cups for to dip the tacos. Shred the meat with two forks in the pot. Assemble as directed.

EMPANADAS DE CARNE MOLIDA

*Serves 6 to 8
(makes 16 empanadas)*

*Total time: 1 hour, plus
2 hours refrigeration time*

Everything is ten times better when wrapped in flaky pastry, especially smoky, spicy beef. These empanadas remind me of walking around the plaza in Mexico, struggling to decide which vendor's fancy-embroidered-napkin-lined basket to choose from. You guessed it—I usually chose the beef! Warm in your hand and comforting in your tummy, they're perfect for taking the edge off a cold winter night, especially when served with Creamy Avocado Salsa (page 231).

Dough:

4 cups all-purpose flour, plus more for kneading and shaping

1 tablespoon baking powder

1 teaspoon salt

½ teaspoon granulated sugar

1 cup (2 sticks) unsalted butter, cut into ½-inch cubes and chilled

Filling:

2 tablespoons canola or other neutral oil

1 pound lean ground beef (90/10)

1 green bell pepper, chopped

1 red bell pepper, chopped

½ small white onion, peeled and chopped (about ⅓ cup)

4 garlic cloves, minced

2 chipotle peppers from canned chipotles in adobo sauce, finely chopped

1½ teaspoons chicken bouillon powder, preferably Knorr

2 teaspoons salt

2 teaspoons dried oregano

2 teaspoons dried thyme

1 teaspoon garlic powder

1 teaspoon ground black pepper

1 large russet potato, peeled and chopped

Make the dough:

In a large bowl, combine the flour, baking powder, salt, and sugar and whisk to combine. Add the butter and, using your hands, gently rub the pieces into the flour mixture until the texture is sandy, about 5 minutes. While mixing with your hands, slowly add up to 1 cup water, ¼ cup at a time, until the dough comes together, about 3 minutes. If the dough seems too dry, add a little more water; if it seems too wet, add more flour, 1 tablespoon at a time. Dust a large surface with flour and knead the dough until smooth and elastic, about 10 minutes. Cover with plastic wrap and refrigerate for 2 hours.

Make the filling:

Heat the oil in a large skillet over medium heat. Add the ground beef, bell peppers, onion, garlic, chipotles, bouillon powder, salt, oregano, thyme, garlic powder, and black pepper. Cook, using a wooden spoon to break the meat into smaller pieces, stirring occasionally, until the meat is no longer pink, about 8 minutes. Add the potatoes and ½ cup water, cover, and cook until the potatoes are fork-tender, about 15 minutes. Transfer to a large bowl. Wipe the skillet clean and set aside.

INGREDIENTS CONTINUE

RECIPE CONTINUES

Assembly:

**1 large egg, beaten with
½ teaspoon water, for egg wash**

**3 cups canola or other neutral oil,
for deep-frying**

**Creamy Avocado Salsa
(page 231), for serving**

To assemble:

Roll out the dough until it's about ¼ inch thick. Use a 6-inch round cookie cutter (or an upside-down bowl and a paring knife) to cut out as many rounds of dough as you can. Gather the scraps, reroll, and cut out more rounds. You should have about 16 rounds of dough.

Spoon 2 tablespoons of the filling into the center of each dough round and fold the dough over to form a half-moon and enclose the filling. Crimp the edges with a fork to seal. Using a pastry brush, brush each empanada with the egg wash.

Set a wire rack over a baking sheet and have it near the stove. Heat the oil in a large skillet with high sides over medium-high heat. To check that the oil is hot enough for frying, dip a wooden toothpick in the oil; if the oil bubbles, it's ready. Working in batches of 2 or 3, fry the empanadas until golden brown on both sides with little bubbles on the surface, about 2 minutes per side. Transfer to the wire rack to drain and repeat with the remaining empanadas.

Arrange the empanadas on a large platter or divide evenly among plates. Serve with salsa on the side.

COCINA TIPS:

- Cold butter is key for a super-flaky crust. I like to cube the butter first and keep it in the fridge until the moment I need it for the dough.

- Empanadas can be fried ahead and cooled to room temperature, then stacked flat on a baking sheet in the freezer until completely frozen, about 2 hours. Transfer the frozen empanadas to freezer-safe bags or containers and freeze for up to 2 months. When ready to use, reheat in a 350°F oven for about 15 minutes.

EDITH'S CHILES RELLENOS

Serves 6

Total time: 2 hours

Meet our family's most in-demand dish: lightly fried, velvety poblano chiles stuffed with creamy, cheesy goodness and smothered with garlicky serrano-tomato sauce. When I was a kid, we would beg for them, but they were a rare treat because they were a bit time-consuming and a labor of love. We'd all have to pitch in, and my job was to peel the poblano chiles and cut the slits for the stuffing. Our family recipe puts a unique twist on the traditional beef picadillo stuffing—we fill the peppers with a luscious blend of mashed potatoes and mozzarella.

Serrano-Tomato Sauce:

7 ripe Roma (plum) tomatoes, cored

3 fresh serrano chiles, stemmed

¼ small white onion, peeled

2 garlic cloves, peeled but whole

1 tablespoon chicken bouillon powder, preferably Knorr

2 teaspoons dried oregano

1 tablespoon canola or other neutral oil

Potato-Cheese Stuffing:

5 russet potatoes, peeled and halved

Salt

2½ cups shredded mozzarella cheese

1 teaspoon garlic powder

1 teaspoon onion powder

Salt, to taste

Chiles Rellenos:

12 large fresh poblano chiles

10 large eggs, separated

¼ cup all-purpose flour, plus more for dredging

2 to 3 cups canola or other neutral oil, for frying

Fresh cilantro, for garnish

Make the serrano-tomato sauce:
In a large pot, combine 4 cups water, the tomatoes, and serranos and bring to a boil over medium-low heat. Reduce the heat to medium and simmer until the tomatoes have broken down and the serranos have softened, about 10 minutes.

Use a slotted spoon to transfer the tomatoes and serranos to a blender. Add the onion, garlic, bouillon powder, and oregano and pulse a few times to break everything down. With the steam vent in the blender top open, blend until the sauce is smooth, about 30 seconds.

Heat the oil in a large skillet over medium heat. Add the sauce and simmer, stirring occasionally, for 10 minutes. Remove from the heat and keep warm. (This can be done a day ahead and reheated, see Tips.) Wipe out the pot.

Make the potato-cheese stuffing:
Place the potatoes in a large pot and add a pinch of salt and cold water to cover. Bring to a boil over medium heat (you can cover with a lid to help it boil faster). Reduce the heat to maintain a simmer and cook, uncovered, until the potatoes are fork-tender, about 45 minutes. Drain the potatoes, transfer to a large bowl, and use a potato masher or ricer to mash until smooth. Stir in the mozzarella, garlic powder, onion powder, and salt to taste and mix to evenly combine. Set aside.

Make the chiles rellenos:
Set a large dry skillet over medium heat. Add the poblanos and use tongs to turn them so they char on every side, about 5 minutes per side. (Alternatively, place them on a baking sheet and broil until

RECIPE CONTINUES

the skins start to blacken, about 5 minutes per side.) Transfer the chiles to a large bowl, cover with a kitchen towel, and let steam for 5 minutes. Carefully remove the chiles from the bowl and set aside until cool enough to handle, then peel off the skin with your fingers without tearing the peppers.

Using a small paring knife, cut a lengthwise slit about 2 inches long in one side of each poblano to make a pocket, taking care not to split them in half. Remove and discard the seeds. Using a teaspoon or your hands, carefully fill each poblano with the potato-cheese stuffing, press the pepper closed, and set aside.

In the bowl of a stand mixer fitted with the whisk attachment (or in a large metal or glass bowl using a handheld mixer), beat the egg whites on low speed for 1 minute. Increase the speed to high and whip until stiff peaks form, about 5 minutes. You should be able to turn the bowl upside down without the egg whites falling out. Add the egg yolks (unbeaten) to the whites and whisk until golden, with barely any white remaining. Using a rubber spatula, gently fold in the flour.

Spread a few cups or so of flour over a large plate for dredging; set aside. Set a wire rack over a large baking sheet and have it near the stove.

Pour 1 inch of canola oil into a large high-sided skillet and heat over medium heat until it reaches 375°F on a deep-fry thermometer. (If you don't have a deep-fry thermometer, dip a wooden toothpick in the oil; if the oil bubbles, it's ready.) Make sure the oil is not smoking; if it is, reduce the heat as needed.

Working in batches of two, dip the stuffed poblanos into the flour to lightly coat both sides. Lightly tap off any excess flour. Using tongs, dip the pepper into the egg batter, carefully place it in the pan, and cook, turning once, until golden brown, about 2 minutes on each side. Transfer the cooked peppers to the wire rack.

To serve:
Spread a layer of the serrano-tomato sauce over the bottom of each of six plates or a large platter. Place the chiles rellenos on top of the sauce, top with more sauce, and garnish with cilantro. Serve immediately.

COCINA TIPS:

- To make the sauce ahead, refrigerate it in a sealed container for up to 2 days. Reheat in a microwave-safe container for about 1 minute before using.

- You can substitute green bell peppers for the poblanos; just add a dash of hot sauce to the filling.

- The peppers can be stuffed (but not battered) and refrigerated in an airtight container 1 day ahead. Bring to room temperature before frying.

- Having the eggs at room temperature will give you the fluffiest whites, resulting in a lighter batter.

- Any leftover mashed potato filling can be used to make Tacos de Papa (page 83).

FLAUTAS

Serves 6 (makes 12 flautas)

Total time: 30 minutes, plus 4 to 6 hours in a slow cooker or 2 to 3 hours on the stovetop

A crunchy and crispy rolled-up tortilla is my happy meal. Just stuff, roll, and fry them up! I'll make a big batch for a party and freeze half so they're always available. Serve these with my Guacamole Salsa Dupe (page 232) or store-bought alongside for dipping. Izzy grabs these flautas and snacks on them while playing with her toys or even watching TV in her bed!

3 pounds boneless, skinless chicken breasts or thighs

2 tablespoons Lawry's seasoned salt

1 (10-ounce) can Ro-Tel diced tomatoes and green chiles

16 ounces mozzarella cheese, shredded

12 (6-inch) flour tortillas, homemade or store-bought

1 cup canola or other neutral oil

For Serving:
Shredded lettuce

Thinly sliced ripe Roma (plum) tomatoes

Creamy Avocado Salsa (page 231)

Pat each chicken dry and season with the Lawry's salt. Place the chicken in a slow cooker. Add 3 cups water and the canned tomatoes and chiles. Cover and cook on high for 4 to 6 hours, until the chicken is tender and shreds easily with a fork.

Transfer the chicken to a bowl with enough of the cooking liquid to keep the meat moist and let cool slightly. When the chicken is cool enough to handle, use two forks or your fingers to shred the meat. Add the mozzarella and stir until evenly combined.

Working on a flat surface, fill each tortilla with ¼ cup of the shredded chicken mixture and roll it up into a tight cigar shape, leaving the ends open. Place the flautas seam-side down on a plate or baking sheet as you work.

Set a wire rack over a baking sheet and have it near the stove. Heat the oil in a large skillet with high

sides over medium heat. To check that the oil is hot enough for frying, dip a wooden toothpick in the oil; if the oil bubbles, it's ready. Working in batches to avoid crowding the pan, carefully add the flautas to the skillet, seam-side down, and cook until golden brown and crispy, about 1 minute per side. Using tongs or a slotted spoon, transfer to the wire rack to drain and repeat with the remaining flautas.

Place two flautas on each plate. Top with lettuce and tomatoes and serve with salsa on the side.

COCINA TIP:

• Alternatively, if using a large Dutch oven or pot, bring the mixture to a boil, then reduce the heat to maintain a simmer. Cover and cook until the chicken is tender and shreds easily with a fork, 2 to 3 hours, stirring midway through. Mix in the mozzarella and assemble as directed.

TOSTADAS WITH PORK RINDS AND TOMATO SALSA

Serves 6

Total time: 15 minutes

These tangy tostadas take me back to the little town outside my abuela's ranch, where we spent many summers. Street cart vendors sell these on every corner in to-go cups to eat while wandering the pretty village. I always keep extra jars of *cueritos* (pickled pork skins) in my pantry so Izzy can share some of my childhood favorites.

5 dried chiles de árbol (use more or less, depending on your spice tolerance), stemmed, split, and seeded

3 ripe Roma (plum) tomatoes, roughly chopped

½ cup roughly chopped fresh cilantro

½ small red onion, roughly chopped (about ¼ cup)

Juice of 1 lime

2 cups mashed Frijoles de Edith (page 171), warmed, or store-bought refried beans

6 tostadas

2 cups cueritos (pickled pork skins)

½ small head green cabbage, thinly sliced

Hot sauce (I prefer Tapatío)

Make the salsa:

In a blender (or food processor), pulse the chiles until finely chopped, about 6 pulses. Add the tomatoes, cilantro, onion, and lime juice and pulse 6 times. The texture of the salsa should still be somewhat coarse, not liquid.

To assemble:

Using a spatula or spoon, evenly spread the beans over each tostada, spreading them to the edges. Top each tostada evenly with the cueritos and cabbage. Place 2 tostadas on each plate. Top with a few spoonfuls of the salsa and a few dashes of hot sauce and serve.

SOPES DE SOY CHORIZO

Serves 6 (makes 12 sopes)

Total time: 1 hour, plus 20 minutes resting time

Non-Spanish-speakers often think sopes must be some kind of soup, so let me clear that up for you: Sopes (pronounced *SO-pays*) are like thicker tortillas that get pinched around the edge to resemble a little pie. I was in charge of the pinching when I was younger; now it's Izzy's job. You can fill them with so many things. This veggie version uses my pinto beans, topped with soy chorizo and garnished with lettuce, tomatoes, queso fresco, pickled onions, and any of the salsas from the Basics chapter (pages 225 to 235).

Dough:

4 cups masa harina (instant corn masa flour), preferably Maseca, plus more as needed

1 teaspoon baking powder

1 teaspoon salt

3½ cups warm water

For Assembly and Serving:

1 cup canola or other neutral oil

11 ounces soy chorizo, loose fresh Mexican chorizo, or your favorite sausage meat (not in links; see Tips)

2 cups mashed Frijoles de Edith (page 171), warmed, or store-bought refried beans

2 cups shredded iceberg lettuce

2 ripe Roma (plum) tomatoes, diced

Crumbled queso fresco

Pickled Onions (page 239)

Salsa Verde (page 235) or store-bought salsa

Make the dough:

In a large bowl, use a wooden spoon to stir together the masa flour, baking powder, and salt. While stirring constantly, slowly drizzle in the warm water, stirring until all the water has been absorbed and the dough feels sticky. Cover the bowl with a kitchen towel and let stand for 20 minutes.

Line a baking sheet with parchment paper or waxed paper.

Divide the dough into 12 equal portions and roll each portion into a ball. If the dough is too sticky to roll, add a tablespoon of masa or more as needed. Line both sides of a tortilla press with plastic wrap (so the tortillas won't stick). Flatten each ball of dough into a 6-inch round and remove the disc from the press using the bottom piece of plastic wrap and transfer to the

prepared baking sheet (see Tips). Reline the press and continue pressing the remaining tortillas.

Heat a comal or cast-iron skillet over medium heat. Place the tortilla on the hot comal or skillet and cook until golden brown on both sides, about 1 minute per side. Return to the tortilla to the baking sheet and, while it's hot, carefully crimp the sides like a pie shell; this is the sope. You can keep a cold, wet towel next to you to moisten and cool your fingers. Repeat with the rest of the tortillas.

Cook the chorizo:

Line a plate with paper towels and have it near the stove. Heat a large deep skillet over medium heat. Add the chorizo and cook, stirring occasionally, until browned and crispy, 8 to 10 minutes. Transfer the chorizo to the paper towels to drain. Wipe the skillet clean.

RECIPE CONTINUES

Assemble and serve the sopes:

Set a wire rack over a baking sheet and have it near the stove. In the same skillet, heat the oil over medium heat until hot. To test the oil, dip a wooden toothpick in the oil; if the oil bubbles, it's ready. Use tongs to carefully place 2 sopes into the pan and cook until golden brown on one side, about 3 minutes. Gently flip and cook until brown on the other side, about 1 minute. Transfer the sopes to the wire rack to drain and repeat with the remaining sopes.

Spoon the beans into the sopes, dividing them evenly. Top evenly with the chorizo. Place 2 sopes on each plate and garnish with lettuce, tomatoes, queso fresco, pickled onions, and salsa.

COCINA TIPS:

- If you can only find chorizo in casings, slice off the tip and squeeze out the sausage meat, then discard the casing.

- If you don't have a tortilla press, you can use the bottom of a large plate. Place a piece of plastic on each side of the dough and press down with the plate to form a 6-inch round.

STUFFED TORTILLAS WITH CHICKEN

Serves 4 to 6 (makes 12 gorditas)

Total time: 2 hours

The best gorditas come from a little spot near my grandmother's ranch, which inspired this recipe. *Gordita* is an endearing Spanish word that means "little chubby one." You'll feel the love, too, when the tender dough puffs up in the oil and cools down for an enormous bite. Use the leftover broth for a soup or pop it in the freezer for later use. Just don't discard it!

Chicken Filling:

2 bone-in, skinless chicken breasts

½ small white onion, peeled

1 head garlic, top one-third sliced off to expose the cloves

2 bay leaves

1 tablespoon chicken bouillon powder, preferably Knorr

1 tablespoon salt

Salsa:

1 teaspoon canola or other neutral oil

14 tomatillos, husked, rinsed, and halved (see Tips on page 47)

½ small white onion, peeled

3 fresh serrano chiles

3 garlic cloves, peeled but whole

1 tablespoon salt

1½ teaspoons chicken bouillon powder, preferably Knorr

Make the chicken filling:

In a large pot, bring 6 cups water to a boil over high heat. Carefully add the chicken, onion, garlic head, bay leaves, bouillon powder, and salt and cook until the chicken is tender and easily falls off the bone, about 45 minutes.

Using tongs, remove the chicken from the broth. Pour the broth through a fine-mesh sieve into a large bowl and discard the bay leaves, onion, and garlic. Save the broth for another use (see Tips). When the chicken is cool enough to handle, pull the meat off the bones. Discard the bones and set the meat aside.

Make the salsa:

Heat the oil in a large skillet over medium heat. Add the tomatillos, onion, serranos, and garlic and cook, stirring frequently, until softened, about 10 minutes. Transfer everything to a blender and add the salt and bouillon powder. With the steam vent in the blender top open, blend on high until smooth, about 45 seconds.

Return the salsa to the skillet and bring to a simmer over medium heat, and cook until slightly thickened, about 5 minutes. Stir in the shredded chicken and simmer until the chicken is warm and has absorbed a little of the sauce, about 5 minutes more, remove from the heat and set aside.

INGREDIENTS CONTINUE

RECIPE CONTINUES

Gorditas:
4 cups masa harina (instant corn flour), preferably Maseca
1 teaspoon baking powder
1 teaspoon salt
3½ cups warm water
1½ cups canola or other neutral oil

For Serving:
Shredded lettuce
Crema Mexicana (see Tips)
Crumbled queso fresco

COCINA TIPS:

- If you can't find crema Mexicana, thin the same amount of sour cream with a little milk.

- The leftover broth can be transferred to an airtight container and frozen for up to 3 months. For a quick soup, thaw the broth in the refrigerator overnight, reheat in a small pot over medium heat, then add your favorite dried noodles or rice and veggies.

- If you don't have a tortilla press, you can use the bottom of a large plate. Place a piece of plastic wrap on both sides of the dough and press down with the plate to form a ½-inch-thick round.

Make the gorditas:
In a large bowl, use a wooden spoon to stir together the masa flour, baking powder, and salt. While stirring constantly, slowly drizzle in the warm water, then stir until all the water has been absorbed and the dough feels sticky. Cover the bowl with a kitchen towel and let stand at room temperature for 20 minutes.

Divide the dough into 12 equal portions and roll each portion into a ball. If the dough is too sticky to roll, add 1 tablespoon of masa flour or more as needed.

Line a large plate or baking sheet with parchment paper or waxed paper. Line a second baking sheet with paper towels and have it near the stove. Line both sides of a tortilla press with plastic wrap (so the tortillas won't stick). Lightly flatten the masa balls to about ½ inch thick. Be sure not to press too hard; these should be thicker than a tortilla. Remove the disc from the press using the bottom piece of plastic wrap. Place the dough on the parchment-lined plate or baking sheet and cover with a kitchen towel (see Tips). Reline the press and continue pressing the remaining tortillas.

Heat a comal or cast iron skillet over medium heat. Toast the tortilla for for 1 to 2 minutes per side. Cover to keep warm. Heat the oil in a deep 10-inch cast-iron skillet over medium heat. Working in batches, place as many gorditas as will fit in the pan and fry on one side until golden brown spots appear across the surface, 2 to 4 minutes. Use tongs to turn the gorditas and fry until spots appear on the other side, 2 to 4 minutes more. Transfer to the paper towels to drain and repeat with the remaining gorditas.

To assemble:
Slice each gordita three-quarters of the way through the center to create a pocket. Divide the shredded chicken mixture between the gorditas and use tongs or a spoon to fill the pocket.

Divide the gorditas evenly among plates. Top the chicken with some lettuce, crema Mexicana, and queso fresco and serve immediately.

PORK RIBS IN CHILES

Serves 4 to 6

Total time: 1 hour

When I started my cooking journey, this recipe was at the top of my to-learn list. At first, I was intimidated, but I built up my courage, and I'm so thankful my mom could take me through step-by-step so I would get it right. While I've never gotten it to taste quite as good as Mom's, my family still goes wild for it. The salsa brings the perfect spice level, and the pork is crisp yet juicy and tender.

Pork Riblets:
½ cup lard or olive oil
1 pound pork riblets (see Tips), cut into 2-inch pieces
1½ teaspoons salt

Sauce:
1 teaspoon canola or other neutral oil
10 tomatillos, husked, rinsed, and halved if large (see Tips, page 47)
1 white onion, peeled and halved
3 fresh serrano chiles
3 garlic cloves, peeled but whole
½ cup finely chopped fresh cilantro
1 to 1½ tablespoons chicken bouillon powder, preferably Knorr

Assembly:
2 tablespoons canola or other neutral oil
1 white potato, peeled and diced

For Serving:
Frijoles de Edith (page 171), warmed, or store-bought refried beans
Crumbled queso fresco
Warm corn tortillas

Make the pork riblets:
Heat the lard in a large skillet over medium heat. Add the pork riblets, season with the salt, and cook, stirring occasionally, until golden brown and crispy, about 15 minutes.

Meanwhile, make the sauce:
Heat the oil in a second large skillet over medium heat. Add the tomatillos, ½ onion, serranos, and garlic and cook, using tongs to constantly keep them moving and turning them on all sides, until they are golden brown and blistered all over, about 10 minutes. If the garlic and onion brown faster than the tomatillos and serranos, remove them from the skillet and transfer them to a blender.

Add the cilantro and 1 tablespoon bouillon powder to the blender, and with the steam vent in the blender top open, blend on high until smooth, about 45 seconds. Taste and adjust the seasoning, adding another ½ tablespoon bouillon powder, if desired.

Chop the remaining onion half. Wipe out the skillet.

To assemble:
Heat the oil in the large skillet over medium heat. Pour in the salsa from the blender and simmer, stirring occasionally, until thickened, about 10 minutes. Add the riblets, the chopped onion, and potato and cook, stirring occasionally, until the potato is fork-tender, 10 to 20 minutes.

Divide evenly among plates. Serve with beans, queso fresco, and warm tortillas.

COCINA TIP:

· Riblets are regular pork ribs that have been cut across the bone into smaller pieces, with alternating meat and bone sections. You may find them labeled as "rib tips." Use a meat cleaver or large sharp knife to cut the pork riblets into 2-inch pieces between the bone segments. All the riblets should be roughly the same size.

MISSISSIPPI POT ROAST

Serves 4 to 6

Total time: 6 to 8 hours in a slow cooker or 3 to 4 hours in the oven

Cooking is about sharing memories, and my husband, Brandon, has fond childhood memories of my mother-in-law Verena's stew. Chuck roast meets ranch dressing, gravy, Worcestershire sauce, and some veggies for a long simmer in a slow cooker or a slow bake in the oven. The house always feels so cozy when there's a roast simmering in broth. Serve this with some bread, rice, or mashed potatoes, because wasting even a drop of that gravy would be a crime!

3 pounds chuck roast

1 tablespoon salt

1 tablespoon ground black pepper

⅓ cup canola or other neutral oil

1½ pounds baby potatoes, halved

4 medium carrots, peeled and each cut into 4 pieces

4 celery stalks, cut into 4 pieces

1 white onion, peeled and quartered

4 garlic cloves, minced

2 cups beef broth

8 tablespoons (1 stick) unsalted butter, sliced

1 (1-ounce) package ranch seasoning

1 (0.88-ounce) package brown gravy mix

1 teaspoon Worcestershire sauce

Crusty bread, mashed potatoes, or Arroz Blanco (page 164), for serving

Pat the chuck roast dry and season all over with the salt and black pepper.

Heat the oil in a large skillet over medium heat. Carefully add the chuck roast and cook until golden brown on one side, about 3 minutes. Flip and cook until golden brown on the second side, about 3 minutes.

Using tongs, transfer the roast to a slow cooker. Add the potatoes, carrots, celery, onion, garlic, broth, butter, ranch seasoning, brown gravy mix, and Worcestershire. Cover and cook on low for about 8 hours or on high for about 6 hours, until the meat is tender and falling apart. Using two forks, shred the meat directly in the slow cooker and mix well.

Evenly divide the stew among bowls. Serve with crusty bread, mashed potatoes, or rice.

COCINA TIP:

- To make this in the oven, preheat the oven to 300°F. Sear the meat in a large Dutch oven or heavy-bottomed pot with a lid as directed, then add all the remaining ingredients. Cover and bake for 3 to 4 hours, stirring midway through, until the meat can be easily shredded with a fork. Shred the meat and serve as directed.

MOLE CON POLLO

Serves 6

Total time: 2 hours

Mole—the complex classic Mexican sauce with a million ingredients—was always very intimidating to me. Containing nuts, chiles, and often chocolate, it seemed too hard to make. This recipe takes me back home to the love my mom would put into her chicken mole. She usually used homemade mole brought to the United States by visiting family, and we'd freeze any leftover magical sauce. Whenever we ran out, Mom would use jarred sauce from the supermarket, throwing in a few extra ingredients to enhance the flavor. Honestly, it was almost just as good, and much more manageable.

Chicken:

4 pounds bone-in, skin-on chicken drumsticks and thighs (see Tips)

½ small white onion, peeled

1 head garlic, top one-third sliced off to expose the cloves

2 bay leaves

2 tablespoons salt

Mole Sauce:

3 tablespoons canola or other neutral oil

2 ripe Roma (plum) tomatoes, halved

½ small white onion, peeled and sliced (about ⅓ cup)

5 garlic cloves, peeled but whole

6 dried guajillo chiles, stemmed, split, and seeded

1 dried pasilla chile, stemmed, split, and seeded

Make the chicken:
In a large pot, bring 10 cups water to a boil over high heat. Add the chicken, onion, garlic head, bay leaves, and salt and boil for 10 minutes, occasionally skimming away any foam that rises to the top. Reduce the heat to medium-low and simmer until the chicken is cooked through and tender, about 35 minutes.

Transfer the chicken to a large bowl or plate. Strain the broth through a fine-mesh sieve set over a separate large bowl; discard the onion, garlic, and bay leaves.

Make the mole sauce:
Heat 1½ tablespoons of the oil in a large skillet over medium heat. Add the tomatoes, onion, and garlic and cook, stirring frequently, until the tomatoes have softened, about 3 minutes. Transfer to a plate and set aside.

Add the guajillo and pasilla chiles to the skillet and cook on all sides until fragrant and just beginning to soften, about 1 minute. Don't cook them too long or the chiles will get bitter. Transfer to the plate with the onion, tomatoes, and garlic.

In a blender, combine the cookies, peanuts, cinnamon stick, oregano, and cloves. Pulse a few times to break everything up and then blend into a fine powder. Add the chiles, tomatoes, onion, garlic, jarred mole sauce, melted chocolate, and 4 cups of the broth. With the steam vent in the blender top open, blend until smooth, about 1 minute.

INGREDIENTS CONTINUE

RECIPE CONTINUES

1 cup crushed Marias Gamesa cookies (about 20 cookies) (see Tips)

2 tablespoons roasted peanuts

½ cinnamon stick

1 teaspoon dried oregano

4 whole cloves

1 (8.25-ounce) jar dark mole sauce (see Tips)

2 ounces Mexican chocolate, preferably Ibarra, melted

Salt (optional)

Arroz Blanco (page 164), for serving

Warm corn tortillas, for serving

In a Dutch oven or wide heavy-bottomed pot, heat the remaining 1½ tablespoons oil over medium heat. Pour the sauce from the blender into the pot along with 2 cups more broth. Cook, stirring frequently with a wooden spoon so the bottom doesn't scorch, until the sauce develops a smooth, creamy consistency, about 30 minutes. If it seems too thick, drizzle in more broth until the desired consistency is reached. Taste and season with salt, as needed.

Add the chicken to the pot and simmer for 20 minutes more.

Evenly divide the mole among six bowls. Serve with rice and warm tortillas.

COCINA TIPS:

- If you can't find Marias Gamesa, you can use graham crackers or vanilla wafers.

- You can use the same weight of bone-in, skin-on thighs instead of a mix of drumsticks and thighs, if preferred.

- Use a mole labeled "dark" or a dark-brown-colored mole. Either will work. What you don't want is a red mole, as that uses different ingredients and will give the dish a different flavor.

BEEF AND VEGETABLE SOUP

Serves 8 to 10　　　　　*Total time: 3 to 4 hours*

Thanks to the beef shank, caldo de res is a hearty soup packed with beef and vegetables in a deep, meaty stock. I start this in the morning so the beef will be tender by dinnertime. The perfect thing about caldos is that they're happy to take any vegetables you have on hand or whatever you're craving, so each batch can be a new variation. Wake this up with a splash of Chile de Árbol Salsa (page 228).

2 pounds chamorro de res (beef shank), precut into 3-inch pieces

2 pounds beef stew meat, cut into 3-inch pieces

2 ears corn, husked and cut into thirds

½ white onion, peeled

½ cup finely chopped fresh cilantro

1 head garlic, top one-third sliced off to expose the cloves

2 mint sprigs

2 tablespoons caldo de res bouillon powder, preferably Knorr

2 tablespoons salt

3 large carrots, peeled, halved lengthwise, and cut crosswise into 1-inch chunks

2 russet potatoes, peeled and cut into 1-inch chunks

2 medium Mexican squash or zucchini, halved lengthwise and cut crosswise into ½-inch-thick half-moons

1 medium chayote (about ½ pound), peeled, seeded, and cut into 1-inch chunks

½ head small green cabbage, quartered

½ cup (about 2 ounces) green beans, trimmed and halved

For Serving:
Sliced fresh jalapeños
Finely chopped fresh cilantro
Lemon wedges

In a large pot, combine the beef shanks, stew meat, corn, onion, cilantro, garlic head, mint, bouillon powder, and salt. Pour in enough water to cover the meat (about 16 cups). Bring to a boil over high heat. Reduce the heat to medium-low and simmer, skimming the foam that rises to the top as needed, until the meat is very tender, 2½ to 3 hours.

Add the carrots, stir, and cook for 6 minutes. Add the potatoes, squash, chayote, cabbage, and green beans and cook, stirring occasionally, until the vegetables are crisp-tender, about 8 minutes.

Divide evenly among bowls. Garnish with jalapeño slices and cilantro and serve with lemon wedges for squeezing.

ANTOJITOS Y ACOMPAÑANTES

Tostilocos

Botana Mexicana con Cueritos /
*Sweet, Spicy, and Pickled
Pork Skins*

Choriqueso

Loaded Carne Asada Nachos

Papas Rellenas

Colifor en Capeada /
*Batter-Fried Cauliflower
in Chipotle Tomato Sauce*

Esquites

Rueditas /
Chile Lime Wheel Chips

Arroz Blanco

Arroz Rojo

Arroz Poblano

Frijoles de Edith

Frijoles Charros /
Cowboy-Style Beans

Macaroni Salad

Potato Wedges

SNACKS AND SIDES

TOSTILOCOS

Serves 2 to 4   *Total time: 20 minutes*

You may have seen these at the store, but in our house, they're called crazy chips because they're a mix of crazy good things like peanuts, tortilla chips, *cueritos* (spicy pickled pork skins), cucumber, jicama, chamoy (see Tips), and—wait for it—tamarind candy! Salty, crunchy, tangy, sweet, and fresh from the veggies—it's got everything. Mouthwatering excitement for your taste buds!

1 (11-ounce) bag Tostitos Salsa Verde tortilla chips

1 medium cucumber, peeled and diced

1 cup diced cueritos (pickled pork skins)

1 cup peeled and diced jicama

1 cup Japanese-style peanuts or dry-roasted salted peanuts (see Tips)

2 tablespoons chamoy (see Tips)

Juice of 1 lime

10 shakes hot sauce (I prefer Tapatío)

⅓ cup crushed dulces tamarind candy, for garnish

In a large bowl, toss together the Tostitos, cucumber, cueritos, jicama, and peanuts. Add the chamoy, lime juice, and hot sauce and use a wooden spoon or tongs to mix until combined.

Transfer to a large serving bowl or individual bowls. Garnish with the crushed candy and serve.

COCINA TIPS:

- Chamoy is a condiment made of pureed dried fruit, chiles, and lime juice.

- Japanese peanuts are coated in wheat flour and soy sauce and deep-fried.

SWEET, SPICY, AND PICKLED PORK SKINS

Serves 1

Total time: 25 minutes

Botanas are Mexican snacks, and you'll see them at almost every street corner of Mexico. This recipe is a delicious explosion of salty, sour, and spicy flavors that are crunchy and juicy in just one bite. The base is fried *duro chicharrón*, a giant wheat chip flavored with chile and lime. Once fried, you top that crispy base with my pinto beans and a layer of crema Mexicana and finish it with a refreshing mix of chopped vegetables, red onions, and *cueritos* (pickled pork skins). But anything would be good on a duro—I often make a lighter version using cabbage and sautéed shrimp.

2 cups canola or other neutral oil, for frying

1 (10-inch-square) duro chicharrón

½ cup mashed Frijoles de Edith (page 171), warmed, or store-bought refried beans

1 cup crema Mexicana (see Tips)

1 cup thinly sliced green cabbage

½ cucumber, peeled and diced

1 ripe Roma (plum) tomato, diced

½ cup thinly sliced red onion

½ cup cueritos (pickled pork skins; see Tips), thinly sliced into rings

½ avocado, thinly sliced

For Serving:

½ lime

Hot sauce (I prefer Tapatío)

Finely chopped fresh cilantro

Line a large plate or small baking sheet with paper towels and have it near the stove. In a deep, wide pot (wider than 10 inches so it can hold the duro), heat the oil over medium heat until almost simmering, about 3 minutes. To test the oil, drop in a ½-inch piece of duro or bread; if it floats up and starts to puff, the oil is ready. Carefully add the duro to the hot oil and cook until it puffs up, about 5 minutes per side, using tongs to flip it halfway through. As it's cooking, use two pairs of tongs to flatten it all around and prevent it from curling up. Using tongs or a slotted spoon, carefully transfer the duro to the paper towels to drain and cool.

Transfer the cooled duro to a plate. Spread the beans on top, followed by the crema. Layer on the cabbage, cucumber, tomato, onion, pickled pork skin, and avocado.

Squeeze the lime juice over the top and add a dash of hot sauce and a sprinkle of cilantro. Serve immediately.

COCINA TIPS:

- If you can't find the duro chicharrón, don't worry! You can substitute 2 cups tortilla chips (or rueditas, which are Mexican fried wheat chips in the shape of wagon wheels). Place the chips on a serving plate and layer the ingredients in the same order on top of them.

- Cueritos are usually sold thinly sliced in jars. You will need to thinly slice them if you can only find bigger pieces.

- If you can't find crema Mexicana, thin the same amount of sour cream with a little milk.

149

CHORIQUESO

Serves 6　　　　　　　　　　　　　　*Total time: 35 minutes*

I don't think many people know about choriqueso, but this cheesy dip with hidden specks of smoky Mexican chorizo is so velvety and melty that they won't forget it once they try it! I love to serve it in a mini cast-iron pan for a bit of a restaurant feel, but it's just as good in a large pan. This molten golden gooey deliciousness is guaranteed to draw a crowd. Use fresh Mexican chorizo sausage if you can find it. This is not a dried Spanish chorizo situation. Feel free to swap in shredded mozzarella if you can't find Oaxaca cheese.

2 fresh poblano chiles

1 pound loose fresh Mexican chorizo or hot Italian sausage meat (not in links; see Tip)

½ small white onion, peeled and chopped (about ⅓ cup)

2 fresh jalapeños, diced

½ cup heavy cream

1½ cups grated Monterey Jack cheese

1½ cups grated queso Oaxaca

Warm corn tortillas, for serving

Heat a large cast-iron pan or skillet over medium heat. Add the poblanos and turn them with tongs so they char on every side, about 5 minutes per side. (Alternatively, place them on a baking sheet and broil until the skins start to blacken, about 5 minutes per side.) Transfer the chiles to a large bowl, cover with a kitchen towel, and let steam for 5 minutes. Carefully remove the chiles from the bowl and set aside until cool enough to handle, then peel them and discard the skin, stems, and seeds. Dice the poblano flesh and set aside.

Preheat the oven to 350°F. Position the top oven rack 3 inches from the broiler.

Heat the skillet over medium heat. Add the chorizo and cook, using a wooden spoon to break it up into smaller pieces and stirring occasionally, until golden brown, about 10 minutes. Add the poblanos, onion, and jalapeños and cook, stirring frequently, until softened, about 3 minutes.

Scoop half the chorizo mixture into a bowl. Stir the heavy cream into the skillet with the remaining chorizo mixture. Sprinkle half of both cheeses over the chorizo. Return the chorizo mixture from the bowl to the pan and top with the remaining cheese. Place on the top oven rack and bake for about 20 minutes, until the cheese melts and bubbles. Switch the oven to broil and broil until the top is speckled with brown spots, 2 to 4 minutes.

Place the hot skillet on a trivet. Serve with warm tortillas.

COCINA TIP:

- If you can only find chorizo in casings, slice off the tip and squeeze out the sausage meat, then discard the casing.

LOADED CARNE ASADA NACHOS

Serves 6 to 8

Total time: 45 minutes, plus 20 minutes and 3 hours marinating time for the Carne Asada

If there's one thing I'm super confident about, it's these loaded nachos. They're Brandon's must-have game-day snack. They take a little prep, which you can do a day in advance, but believe me, they are worth it. Start by making my Carne Asada (page 108), then my Pinto Beans (page 171), and my Favorite Guacamole (page 236). That's when you can start carefully layering chips, cheese, and some sour cream (I'm obsessed with making these nachos pretty!). And honestly, if you use canned refried beans or store-bought guac, they'll still be incredible!

Chips:
2 cups canola or other neutral oil, for frying
30 corn tortillas, cut into quarters
Salt

Nacho cheese:
1 tablespoon unsalted butter
3 tablespoons all-purpose flour
3 cups half-and-half, at room temperature
2 cups shredded sharp cheddar cheese
1 teaspoon salt

Assembly:
2 cups mashed Frijoles de Edith (page 171), warmed, or store-bought refried beans
2 cups bite-size pieces Carne Asada (page 108)
1 cup sour cream
Edith's Favorite Guacamole (page 236) or store-bought

COCINA TIP:

- It's important to constantly whisk and stir while making the nacho cheese sauce to prevent lumps from forming.

Make the chips:
Set a wire rack over a baking sheet or line a large baking sheet with paper towels and have it near the stove. Heat the oil in a large skillet with high sides over medium-high heat. To check that the oil is hot enough for frying, dip a wooden toothpick in the oil; if the oil bubbles, it's ready. Working in batches to avoid crowding the skillet, add a handful of tortilla quarters at a time. Cook, using a slotted spoon to turn them occasionally in the oil, until golden brown and crisp, about 2 minutes. (If the chips brown too quickly, reduce the heat and allow the oil to cool for a minute before continuing.) With a slotted spoon, transfer the chips to the rack or paper towels and sprinkle them with salt while still warm. Repeat with the remaining tortilla quarters.

Make the nacho cheese:
Melt the butter in a large pot over medium heat. Add the flour and whisk constantly until a thick paste forms and the flour is lightly browned and toasted, about 1 minute. While whisking constantly, slowly pour in the half-and-half and cook until warmed through and slightly thickened, about 6 minutes. Reduce the heat to low and add the cheddar, one handful at a time, stirring constantly with a wooden spoon or silicone spatula. Cook until the cheese has fully melted and the sauce is smooth, about 2 minutes. Stir in the salt.

To assemble and serve:
Spread all the chips over an extra-large pan or platter. Top with layers of nacho cheese, beans, carne asada, sour cream, and guacamole. Enjoy!

PAPAS RELLENAS

Serves 6
(makes 12 stuffed potatoes)

Total time: 1 hour

I don't know anyone who can pass up this dish. Mashed potatoes with cheese and ham, covered in bread crumbs, flattened, and fried—yum. We think they're the perfect late-afternoon snack to enjoy before heading out to a movie or when friends come over, catching up over glasses of wine in the kitchen as I fry up a fresh batch. We always reach for ranch dressing, along with lettuce, tomato, and a slice of lemon for serving.

3½ pounds large Yukon Gold potatoes, peeled

Salt

12 slices deli ham, finely diced

1 cup shredded mozzarella cheese

1 large egg, beaten

⅓ cup fine dried bread crumbs

2 tablespoons all-purpose flour, plus more as needed

1½ cups canola or other neutral oil, for shallow-frying, or more as needed

For Serving:
Shredded romaine lettuce

Sliced tomatoes

Lemon slices

Ranch dressing

Place the potatoes in a large pot and add 1½ teaspoons salt and enough water to just cover them. Cover the pot and bring to a boil over high heat. Uncover, reduce the heat to maintain a simmer, and cook until the potatoes are fork-tender, about 20 minutes. Drain the potatoes and transfer to a large bowl. Using a potato masher, mash the potatoes until they are slightly chunky, with some small intact pieces, not totally creamy.

Fold the ham, mozzarella, egg, bread crumbs, and 1 tablespoon salt into the mashed potatoes until evenly combined. Divide the mixture into 12 equal portions, form each portion into a ball, and flatten each into a disc about 1 inch thick. Spread the flour over a plate and evenly dredge each disc on all sides in the flour, then place on a large plate or baking sheet until ready to fry.

Set a wire rack over a baking sheet or line a large baking sheet with paper towels and have it near the stove. Heat the oil in a large skillet with high sides over medium heat until hot but not smoking. Working in batches to avoid crowding the pan, carefully add the potato patties and cook until a golden brown crust forms on the bottom, 3 to 5 minutes. Using tongs or a spatula, carefully flip the patties and cook until golden brown on the other side, about 2 minutes more. Add more oil as needed. Transfer to the rack or paper towels to cool and repeat with the remaining patties. Once cool, season the patties with a pinch of salt.

Place some lettuce on each of six plates and top with sliced tomato. Top with 2 potato patties and garnish with sliced lemons and ranch dressing and serve.

BATTER-FRIED CAULIFLOWER IN CHIPOTLE TOMATO SAUCE

Serves 4

Total time: 50 minutes

I discovered this traditional cauliflower recipe courtesy of my husband's great-aunt. The florets are crisp on the outside and soft and fluffy on the inside—irresistible when smothered in a smoky, creamy chipotle tomato sauce. Served with Arroz Blanco (page 164), they're an impressive vegetarian starter, or you can double the recipe for a main dish. These may even get your kids to try cauliflower!

Cauliflower:
1 head cauliflower, separated into large florets
Salt

Chipotle Tomato Sauce:
7 ripe Roma (plum) tomatoes, cored but left whole
2 fresh serrano chiles, left whole
¼ white onion, peeled
2 garlic cloves, peeled but whole
1 canned chipotle pepper in adobo sauce
1 teaspoon chicken bouillon powder, preferably Knorr
½ teaspoon dried oregano
1 tablespoon canola or other neutral oil

Batter:
6 large eggs, separated
2 tablespoons all-purpose flour
3 cups canola or other neutral oil, for frying
Salt and ground black pepper

For Serving:
Crumbled queso fresco
Chopped fresh cilantro
Arroz Blanco (page 164)

Cook the cauliflower:
Bring 3 to 4 inches of water to a simmer in a large pot over medium heat. (The pot should be large enough to fit a steamer basket or metal colander inside.) Carefully place the steamer basket inside the pot, making sure the water doesn't touch the bottom of the basket. Place the cauliflower in the basket, sprinkle with salt, cover, and steam until tender but not soft, about 6 minutes. Transfer to a bowl to cool. Rinse the pot and set aside.

Make the chipotle tomato sauce:
Fill a large bowl with ice and water. Fill the pot you used for the cauliflower halfway with water and bring to a boil over high heat. Add the tomatoes and serranos and boil until the tomato skins ares loose, about 10 minutes. Transfer to the ice bath until cool enough to handle. (I prefer to have the skin slightly softened, but you don't have to peel the tomato.) Wipe the pot dry.

Using a slotted spoon, transfer the tomatoes and serranos to a blender and add the onion, garlic, chipotle, bouillon powder, and oregano. Pulse a few times to chop the vegetables, then blend on high until smooth, about 45 seconds.

Heat the oil in the same pot over medium heat. Pour in the sauce and bring to a boil, stirring occasionally. Reduce the heat and simmer while you fry the cauliflower. (The sauce can be made a day ahead and reheated. See Tip.)

Make the batter:
In the bowl of a stand mixer fitted with the whisk attachment (or in a large metal or glass bowl using a handheld mixer), beat the egg whites on low speed for 1 minute. Increase the speed to high and whip until stiff peaks form, about

RECIPE CONTINUES

5 minutes. You should be able to turn the bowl upside down without the egg whites falling out. Using a fork, whisk the egg yolks, then, with a rubber spatula, gently fold them into the whites until barely any white shows. Gently fold in the flour.

Set a wire rack over a large baking sheet and have it near the stove. Heat the oil in a large skillet over medium heat. To test the oil, dip a wooden toothpick in the oil; if the oil bubbles, it's ready. Make sure the oil is not smoking; if it is, lower the heat. Working in batches to avoid crowding the pan, dip the cauliflower florets into the batter, shake off any excess using tongs or a slotted spoon, and carefully add

them to the oil. Cook, using a large slotted spoon or silicone spatula to turn the florets as they fry, until the batter is golden and crisp, about 4 minutes. Transfer the cauliflower to the wire rack to drain and repeat with the remaining cauliflower. Season with salt and pepper to taste.

Increase the heat under the skillet with the tomato sauce to medium. Add the fried cauliflower to the sauce and cook, stirring occasionally, for 5 minutes to meld the flavors.

Divide the cauliflower evenly among four plates. Garnish with queso fresco and cilantro and serve with rice.

COCINA TIP:

- Store the sauce in a jar or other airtight container, and refrigerate for up to 5 days or freeze for up to 2 months.

ESQUITES

Serves 5   *Total time: 20 minutes*

Mexican corn is a beloved street food, either sold as elotes—charred cobs slathered in mayo and rolled in Cotija cheese, chile, and cilantro—or (like this recipe) as esquites, a salad in a cup. Today, esquites has made its way to menus all over the US, and it's a cool way to add a punch of flavor to sweet corn. Playing with tradition, my version simmers corn kernels in chicken bouillon until the corn absorbs almost all the broth. It's pretty when served in a glass with a dollop of mayo, a sprinkle of tangy Cotija, a big squeeze of lime juice, and a generous shake of Tajín, a lime-salt-chile seasoning blend. You can use veggie bouillon powder to make it completely vegetarian.

Esquites:
10 ears yellow corn, husked and kernels sliced off, or 10 cups thawed frozen corn kernels

4 tablespoons (½ stick) unsalted butter

1 tablespoon chicken bouillon powder, preferably Knorr

For Serving:
1 cup mayonnaise

⅔ cup crumbled Cotija cheese

Roughly chopped fresh cilantro

Tajín (see Tip), for sprinkling

Lime wedges

Make the esquites:
In a large pot, combine the corn and butter and cook over medium heat, stirring, until the butter melts and fully coats the corn. Pour in 3½ cups water, add the bouillon powder, and stir until the bouillon has dissolved. Increase the heat to high and bring to a boil. Reduce the heat to medium-low and simmer until the corn becomes tender and has absorbed most of the liquid, about 10 minutes. Drain the corn.

Divide the corn evenly among five bowls. Top each with 3 tablespoons of the mayonnaise and 2 tablespoons of the Cotija. Sprinkle with cilantro and Tajín and serve with lime wedges for squeezing.

COCINA TIP:

- Tajín is a store-bought Mexican spice mix made of lime, mild dried chiles, and salt. Add extra lime juice, hot sauce, and salt if you can't find it.

CHILE LIME WHEEL CHIPS

Serves 1

Total time: 15 minutes, plus 15 minutes for cooling

Rueditas remind me so much of Mexico, where the ladies in the plaza fry these crispy puffed wheat-flour-based wagon wheels to serve in a bag with lime and chiles. There are store-bought seasoned rueditas, already flavored with chile and lime, but I like to make my own by starting with unfried wagon wheels. You can find these in a Mexican grocery store or online.

2 cups canola or other neutral oil, for frying

1 cup unfried plain rueditas

Juice of 1 lime

Hot sauce, preferably Tapatío

Line a plate with paper towels and have it near the stove. Heat the oil in a large skillet over medium heat until hot but not smoking. To test the oil, dip a wooden toothpick in the oil; if the oil bubbles, it's ready.

Carefully add the rueditas and cook until they puff up and the orange-colored spots disappear, about 1 minute. Using tongs or a slotted spoon, transfer them to the paper towels to cool for about 15 minutes.

To serve:

In a large serving bowl, combine the rueditas, lime juice, and hot sauce to taste and toss until well coated. Serve immediately. Store any leftovers in an airtight container unrefrigerated, for a few days.

ARROZ BLANCO

Serves 6   *Total time: 45 minutes*

We can't get enough rice in our family! This is the basic recipe and the same method I use for my Arroz Rojo (page 167) and Arroz Poblano (page 168). Remember these two crucial rules to make the fluffiest rice: 1) You must rinse the rice carefully to remove the excess starch. 2) Always put parchment paper under the lid. I prefer fragrant jasmine rice, but any white rice will benefit from these rules.

1 tablespoon canola or other neutral oil

2 cups uncooked jasmine rice, rinsed (see Tips)

Salt and ground black pepper

Cut a piece of parchment paper in a round to fit inside a large lidded skillet (see Tips). Heat the oil in the skillet over medium heat. Add the rice and toast until golden brown, 2 to 4 minutes.

Reduce the heat to medium-low. Add 4 cups water, top with the parchment round, and cover with a lid. Cook the rice for 10 minutes, then reduce the heat to low and cook until all the liquid has been absorbed and the rice is tender, about 25 minutes more. Remove from the heat.

Season to taste with salt and black pepper. Fluff the rice with a fork before serving.

COCINA TIPS:

- I use a 3-quart, 10½-inch lidded skillet.
- To rinse rice, place it in a fine-mesh sieve and rinse under cool running water until the water runs clear, about 2 minutes. Shake to drain any excess water.
- The parchment helps steam the rice by trapping the moisture and causing it to travel back down into the rice. This creates fluffy and tender rice every time.
- Don't worry about the toasted brown bits of rice— they're delicious!

ARROZ ROJO

Serves 6   *Total time: 50 minutes*

Rice went with literally every meal we had growing up. My mother's technique is the best, and with seven million TikTok viewers showing their approval, I can't argue! I asked her to teach me her method right after Brandon and I were married, and it took me almost four years to perfect it. I like to think I went through the struggle to make it easy for you. While my mom's perfect rice goes with almost everything in this book, I love it as a snack with banana slices and a bolillo, a classic Mexican roll that's crusty on the outside and soft on the inside. It's also a hit with crispy Milanesa de Res (page 107).

2 ripe Roma (plum) tomatoes, halved

¼ green bell pepper, halved

¼ small white onion, peeled and roughly chopped

2 garlic cloves, peeled but whole

1 tablespoon chicken bouillon powder, preferably Knorr

¼ teaspoon ground cumin

3 tablespoons canola or other neutral oil

2 cups uncooked jasmine rice, rinsed (see Tips)

In a blender, combine the tomatoes, bell pepper, onion, garlic, bouillon powder, cumin, and 2 cups water and blend until smooth, about 30 seconds.

Cut a piece of parchment paper in a round to fit inside a large lidded skillet (see Tips). Heat the oil in the skillet over medium heat. Add the rice and cook, stirring frequently, until lightly golden brown and translucent, about 10 minutes.

Reduce the heat to medium-low. Add the sauce and 2 cups water (you should have a total of 4 cups liquid; add more water as needed). Top with the parchment round and cover with a lid. Cook the rice for 10 minutes, then reduce the heat to low and cook until all the liquid has been absorbed and the rice is tender, about 25 minutes more.

Fluff the rice with a fork before serving.

COCINA TIPS:

- I use a 3-quart, 10½-inch lidded skillet.

- To rinse the rice, place it in a fine-mesh sieve and rinse under cool running water until the water runs clear, about 2 minutes. Shake to drain any excess water.

- The parchment helps steam the rice by trapping the moisture and causing it to travel back down into the rice. This creates fluffy, tender rice every time.

- Don't worry about the toasted brown bits of rice—they're delicious!

ARROZ POBLANO

Serves 6

Total time: 1 hour

This authentic Mexican side dish has become one of Izzy's favorites because the green rice reminds her of *Green Eggs and Ham*! Green bell peppers will work just fine but the poblanos have more personality, especially when charred. It's another reason—besides Chiles Rellenos (page 123)—to stock your fridge with poblanos. This herbal and peppery rice is delicious with roast chicken or Milanesa de Res (page 107).

2 fresh poblano chiles

¼ small white onion, peeled

2 garlic cloves, peeled but whole

1½ cups fresh cilantro

2 tablespoons chicken bouillon powder, preferably Knorr

Salt and ground black pepper

1 tablespoon canola or other neutral oil

2 cups uncooked jasmine rice, rinsed (see Tips)

1 (15.25-ounce) can corn kernels, drained and rinsed

Heat a large skillet over medium heat. Add the poblanos and turn them with tongs so they char on all sides, about 5 minutes per side. (Alternatively, place them on a baking sheet and broil until the skins start to blacken, about 5 minutes per side.) Transfer the chiles to a large bowl, cover with a kitchen towel, and let steam for 5 minutes. Carefully remove the chiles from the bowl and set aside until cool enough to handle, then peel them and discard the skin, stems, and seeds.

Transfer the peeled poblanos to a blender and add the onion, garlic, cilantro, bouillon powder, a pinch each of salt and black pepper, and 4 cups water. With the steam vent in the blender top open, blend on medium-high until smooth, about 1 minute.

Cut a piece of parchment paper in a round to fit inside a large lidded skillet (see Tips). Heat the oil in the skillet over medium heat. Add the rice and toast until golden brown, 2 to 4 minutes. Add the sauce from the blender along with the corn and reduce the heat to low. Top the rice with the parchment round, cover with the lid, and cook until the rice has absorbed the liquid and is tender, 25 to 30 minutes.

Fluff the rice with a fork before serving.

COCINA TIPS:

- I use a 3-quart, 10½-inch lidded skillet.

- To rinse the rice, place it in a fine-mesh sieve and rinse it under cool running water until the water runs clear, about 2 minutes. Shake to drain any excess water.

- The parchment helps steam the rice by trapping the moisture and causing it to travel back down into the rice. This creates fluffy, tender rice every time.

- Don't worry about the toasted brown bits of rice—they're delicious!

FRIJOLES DE EDITH

Serves 6

Total time: 15 minutes prep plus 6 to 8 hours (or up to overnight) in a slow cooker or 2 hours on the stovetop in a Dutch oven

These delicious beans are the perfect side dish to pretty much anything (see: almost every recipe, lol). I prefer to use dried beans over canned, but I never remember to soak them the night before. Making them in the slow cooker like my mother does allows me to skip that annoying step. I know it's not the traditional way, but sometimes kitchen appliances help you manage your time. If you don't have a slow cooker, you can make them on the stovetop . . . but you must soak them if you're using that method!

1 pound dried pinto beans (about 2 cups), rinsed, drained, and picked over for stones

1 cup finely chopped fresh cilantro, plus more for garnish

½ white onion, peeled

1 head garlic, top one-third sliced off to expose the cloves

2 bay leaves

2 tablespoons chicken bouillon powder, preferably Knorr

1 teaspoon ground cumin

For Serving (optional):
Crumbled queso fresco
Finely chopped white onion
Finely chopped fresh jalapeños
Warm corn or flour tortillas

In a 6-quart or larger slow cooker, combine the pinto beans, cilantro, onion, garlic, bay leaves, bouillon powder, and cumin. Pour in enough water to just cover the ingredients, about 5 quarts (20 cups). Cover and cook on high for 6 to 8 hours or on low for 10 to 12 hours (or up to overnight), until softened and tender.

Using tongs or a slotted spoon, remove and discard the onion, garlic, and bay leaf before serving.

Divide the beans evenly among shallow bowls. Top with queso fresco, onion, and jalapeños and serve with warm tortillas, if using.

COCINA TIPS:

- If you don't have a slow cooker, you can use a Dutch oven on the stovetop. Soak the beans overnight in an uncovered pot with enough cool water to cover. Drain and rinse well in a colander. In the Dutch oven, combine the soaked beans, garlic, onion, bay leaves, bouillon powder, cumin, cilantro, and just enough water to cover the ingredients (about 5 quarts). Bring to a boil over high heat, cover, and reduce the heat to low. Simmer until softened and tender, about 2 hours, stirring midway through.

- For a vegetarian version, use vegetable bouillon powder.

COWBOY-STYLE BEANS

Serves 4 to 6

Total time: 2 hours 30 minutes

I first had these at a friend's party and knew I had to make them my way. These beans, cooked low and slow, are hearty enough to satisfy ravenous *rancheros* (ranchers) around the fire after a long day. Now, I'm not rustling cattle, just rustling up dinner for Izzy and her dad, haha, and I'm pretty sure they love all the bacon, chorizo, and hot dogs I add as much as, or more than, the beans. I'll usually make this during the day while Izzy's at school, cooking the beans straight from dried since I have the time. The two hours it takes to soften them up and pull all those flavors together is just enough time to get organized with the rest of my day before she comes home.

1 pound dried pinto beans (about 2 cups), rinsed, drained, and picked over for stones

1 small white onion, peeled and halved

1 head garlic, top one-third sliced off to expose the cloves

1 tablespoon salt

½ pound bacon (about 8 slices), cut into ¼-inch-wide pieces

3 hot dogs, cut into ¼-inch-thick rounds

½ pound loose fresh Mexican chorizo (not in links; see Tip)

2 ripe Roma (plum) tomatoes, finely diced

2 fresh jalapeños, finely diced

½ cup finely chopped cilantro, plus more for garnish

In a large soup pot, combine the pinto beans, ½ onion, the garlic, salt, and 8 cups water and bring to a boil over medium heat. Reduce the heat to low and cook, stirring occasionally, until the beans are tender, about 2 hours. Dice the remaining onion half and set aside.

Heat a large skillet over medium-high heat. Add the bacon and cook, stirring frequently, until crispy, about 8 minutes. Add the hot dogs and chorizo and cook, stirring occasionally, until browned, about 4 minutes. Add the diced onion, tomatoes, and jalapeños and cook, stirring frequently, until the vegetables have softened, about 4 minutes.

Stir the meat mixture and cilantro into the pot of beans. Simmer, stirring occasionally, until slightly thickened, about 10 minutes.

Divide evenly among bowls and garnish with more cilantro and serve.

COCINA TIP:

- If you can only find chorizo in casings, slice off the tip and squeeze out the sausage meat, then discard the casing.

MACARONI SALAD

Serves 8

Total time: 30 minutes, plus 2 to 4 hours refrigeration time

This is one of my most popular viral recipes. You'll find a version of macaroni salad at almost every Mexican picnic or potluck. I love the combination of sweet corn, ham, and the crunch of carrots and celery, all tied together with a creamy apple cider vinegar mayo. A sprinkle of sugar softens the vinegar's sourness and pulls all the ingredients together.

1 pound elbow macaroni

2 bay leaves

Salt

1½ cups mayonnaise

¼ cup whole milk

1 tablespoon apple cider vinegar

1 tablespoon granulated sugar

Ground black pepper

16 ounces cooked ham, diced

3 celery stalks, chopped

1 cup shredded carrots (about 2 medium)

½ cup, drained and rinsed canned corn kernels

Bring a 4-quart pot of water to a boil over high heat. Add the macaroni, bay leaves, and a generous pinch of salt and cook until the pasta is fully cooked and slightly soft (according to the package directions), stirring occasionally. Drain, discard the bay leaves, and set aside.

Meanwhile, in a large bowl, whisk together the mayonnaise, milk, vinegar, sugar, 2 teaspoons salt, and a big pinch of black pepper.

Add the cooked pasta to the mayo dressing; along with the ham, celery, carrots, and corn and toss until well combined. Taste and adjust the seasoning. Cover with plastic wrap and refrigerate for 2 to 4 hours before serving.

Transfer the salad to a large serving bowl and serve chilled.

POTATO WEDGES

Serves 6

Total time: 45 minutes in an air fryer or 1 hour in the oven

I first made this recipe to see if I could make tasty potato wedges in an air fryer, and guess what happened? It went viral with five million likes! But don't panic if you don't have one—they won't disappoint when roasted in the oven instead. Small creamer potatoes are cut into half-moons and blanketed with Italian herbs and olive oil. They're now our must-have side dish for burgers!

15 to 18 small creamer potatoes, halved

Extra-virgin olive oil

1 tablespoon salt

1½ tablespoons ground black pepper

1 tablespoon Italian seasoning

2 teaspoons sweet paprika

1 teaspoon garlic powder

1 teaspoon onion powder

½ teaspoon dried basil

Ketchup, for serving

Preheat an air fryer or the oven to 400°F. Line a sheet pan with paper towels.

Place the potatoes in a large bowl and add enough water to cover. Let stand for about 15 minutes to pull some of the starch out of the potatoes.

Drain the potatoes and transfer them to the paper towel–lined sheet pan to dry. Wipe the bowl dry. Return the potatoes to the bowl and drizzle with olive oil, then sprinkle with the salt, black pepper, Italian seasoning, paprika, garlic powder, onion powder, and basil. Toss to coat the potatoes thoroughly. If using an air fryer, spread the potatoes in a single layer in an air fryer tray or basket. If using the oven, dry the sheet pan and line it with parchment paper, then spread the potatoes over it in a single layer.

Air-fry or roast the potatoes until browned and crispy, 20 to 35 minutes in the air fryer or 40 to 45 minutes in the oven.

Transfer the potatoes to a large platter and serve with ketchup.

POSTRES Y BEBIDAS

Flan / *Caramel Custard*

Chocoflan Bundt Cake

Nutella Tres Leches

Lemon Blueberry Loaf Cake

Limón Carlota /
No-Bake Lime Cheesecake

Mexican Tiramisu

Budín de Pan / *Bread Pudding*

Arroz con Leche / *Rice Pudding*

Buñuelos

Churros

Chocolate Caliente Mexicano

Quesadilla Salvadoreña /
Sweet Cheese Quesadilla

Fresas con Crema

Diablitos /
Devilishly Delicious Ice Pops

Paletas de Fresas

Agua de Limón con Pepino y Chia /
*Cucumber, Lime, and Chia
Smoothie*

Agua de Jamaica / *Hibiscus Cooler*

Horchata

Atole Chocolate /
Chocolate and Corn Pudding

DESSERTS AND DRINKS

CARAMEL CUSTARD

Serves 6

Total time: 1 hour 15 minutes, plus 4 hours or up to overnight chilling

Here's my recipe for flan without fear! My secret to getting it super smooth and silky is to add cream cheese to the usual canned evaporated and condensed milks, which helps stabilize the mixture so there's no risk of the custard breaking while amping it up to the ultimate creaminess at the same time. The caramel topping can be tricky, too, but never fear. I'm here for you! Read my tips on working with caramel before you start, and you'll be golden (pun intended). This needs to chill for at least 4 hours, and IMO tastes best cold, sprinkled with crumbled Marias Gamesa cookies.

Baking spray

1 (14-ounce) can sweetened condensed milk

1 (12-ounce) can evaporated milk

8 ounces cream cheese, at room temperature

4 large eggs

1 tablespoon vanilla extract

Pinch of salt

1 cup granulated sugar

Berries, for serving

Crumbled Marias Gamesa cookies, for garnish

Preheat the oven to 325°F. Coat an 8-inch round cake pan with baking spray.

In a blender, combine the condensed milk, evaporated milk, cream cheese, eggs, vanilla, and salt and blend until smooth, about 45 seconds. Scrape down the sides of the blender if necessary so everything is fully incorporated.

Heat a medium saucepan over medium heat. Add the sugar and cook, stirring constantly and scraping down the sides of the pan to prevent burning, until fully melted and dark gold in color, 8 to 10 minutes. Carefully and quickly pour the hot caramel into the prepared cake pan, tilting the pan to spread the caramel evenly over the bottom before it sets (be careful, the pan and the caramel will be hot!). Let cool for 2 minutes, then pour in the flan mixture.

Place the flan in a large baking or roasting pan and place the nested pans on a pulled-out oven rack. Pour in enough lukewarm water to come three-quarters of the way up the side of the flan pan. Bake for about 55 minutes, until the custard is set around the edges but still jiggly in the center. Carefully remove the nested pans from the oven and transfer the flan pan to a wire rack. Let cool for 1 hour.

Invert a large plate over the cake pan and carefully flip the pan and plate over to release the flan onto the plate. If it does not slide out immediately, give it a few slaps on top until you hear it release from the pan. You can also try carefully running a table knife around the edge of the flan to help it release. Refrigerate, uncovered, for at least 4 hours or up to overnight before serving.

Slice the flan and spoon some of the sauce over each serving. Serve with berries, and garnish with crumbled cookies.

COCINA TIPS:

- Hot sugar is dangerous, so be extra careful when making caramel! I always have a bowl of ice water standing by in case of burns.

- Be patient and don't take your eyes off the sugar. It will take a while to melt, but once it starts, it will begin to brown and turn dark very quickly, and can go from brown to burnt in a matter of seconds.

- Make sure you use a heatproof silicone spoon or spatula to stir the sugar. The last thing you need is for bits of rubber or plastic to melt into your caramel!

CHOCOFLAN BUNDT CAKE

Serves 8

Total time: 1 hour 15 minutes, plus 2 hours refrigeration time

Is it a cake? Is it custard? It's both, and it's choco-licious. This recipe makes it totally possible to have everything you want in one dreamy cake. Serve a slice with a spoonful of mixed berries, and you're in heaven. If it were up to me, I'd hide this and eat it all by myself, but Izzy would be furious, so I can't do that!

Flan:

Baking spray for the pan

1 cup granulated sugar

1 (14-ounce) can sweetened condensed milk

8 ounces cream cheese, at room temperature

1 (12-ounce) can evaporated milk

4 large eggs

1 tablespoon vanilla extract

¼ teaspoon salt

Make the flan:

Preheat the oven to 425°F. Lightly grease a 10-cup Bundt cake pan with melted butter or baking spray.

Heat a medium saucepan over medium heat. Add the sugar and cook, stirring constantly and scraping down the sides of the pan to prevent burning, until fully melted and dark gold in color, about 8 to 10 minutes. Carefully and quickly pour the hot caramel into the prepared Bundt pan, tilting the pan to spread the caramel evenly over the bottom before it sets (be careful, the pan and the caramel will be hot!).

Combine the condensed milk, cream cheese, evaporated milk, eggs, vanilla, and salt in a blender, and blend on high until smooth, about 1 minute. Pour the cream cheese mixture into the prepared pan over the caramel. It should only come halfway up the side of the pan in order to leave room for the cake batter to be poured on top.

Place the Bundt pan in a large baking pan or roasting pan and place the nested pans on a pulled-out oven rack. Pour 2 inches of water into the roasting pan. Bake for about 25 minutes, until the flan is set on top but still jiggles when shaken. Remove from the oven and set the Bundt pan on a wire rack while you make the cake batter. Keep the oven on and reserve the water bath.

INGREDIENTS CONTINUE

RECIPE CONTINUES

Cake Batter:

1¾ cups all-purpose flour, sifted

1¾ cups granulated sugar

¾ cup unsweetened cocoa powder

2 teaspoons baking powder

1 teaspoon baking soda

1 teaspoon salt

1 cup whole milk

8 tablespoons (1 stick) unsalted butter, melted

½ cup sour cream

3 large eggs

1 teaspoon vanilla extract

A mix of berries (strawberries, blackberries, blueberries) or your favorite fruit, cut up, for serving

Make the cake batter:

In a large bowl, whisk together the flour, sugar, cocoa powder, baking powder, baking soda, and salt. In a medium bowl, whisk together the milk, melted butter, sour cream, eggs, and vanilla until smooth. Pour the milk mixture into the flour mixture and use a spatula to fold until well incorporated.

Pour the cake batter on top of the baked flan and return it to the water bath, adding more water if needed for a depth of 2 inches. Bake for 35 to 40 minutes, until a toothpick inserted into the center of the cake comes out clean. Let the cake cool on a wire rack for at least 1 hour.

Flip the cooled cake out onto a serving plate. Refrigerate uncovered for 1 to 2 hours before serving.

Slice the cake and top with a few spoonfuls of berries or assorted fruit of choice and serve.

COCINA TIPS:

- Hot sugar is dangerous, so be extra careful when making caramel! I always have a bowl of ice water standing by in case of burns.

- Be patient and don't take your eyes off the sugar. It will take a while to melt, but once it starts, it will begin to brown and turn dark very quickly, and can go from brown to burnt in a matter of seconds.

- Make sure you use a heatproof silicone spoon or spatula to stir the sugar. The last thing you need is for bits of rubber or plastic to melt into your caramel!

NUTELLA TRES LECHES CAKE

Serves 10 to 12

Total time: 1 hour, plus 2 hours refrigeration time

Tres leches is a beloved light sponge cake traditionally made with three kinds of milk: condensed, evaporated, and whole. But since I can't get enough chocolate, I've taken this dessert deeper into deliciousness with a chocolate-hazelnut soak that seeps down into the little holes in the light and airy cake, saturating it with sweetness. And I don't stop there, either—a chocolate whipped cream topping makes it unforgettable!

Cake:
Baking spray, for the pan
1 (13.25-ounce) box chocolate cake mix, preferably Betty Crocker Favorites Super Moist Chocolate Fudge
1¼ cups whole milk
1 cup (2 sticks) unsalted butter, melted
3 large eggs

Soak:
1 (14-ounce) can sweetened condensed milk
1 (12-ounce) can evaporated milk
1 cup whole milk
½ cup Nutella or other chocolate-hazelnut spread

Whipped Cream Topping:
2 cups heavy cream
3 tablespoons unsweetened cocoa powder
1½ teaspoons granulated sugar
Nutella, warmed, for drizzling
5 Marias Gamesa or Oreo cookies, crushed, for garnish

Make the cake:
Preheat the oven to 350°F. Lightly grease a 9 x 13-inch baking pan with baking spray.

In a large bowl, whisk together the cake mix, milk, melted butter, and eggs until smooth. Pour the batter into the prepared pan.

Bake until a cake tester inserted into the center comes clean, about 35 minutes. Let the cake cool on a wire rack for at least 20 minutes.

Make the soak:
In the bowl of a stand mixer fitted with the whisk attachment (or in a large glass or metal bowl using a handheld mixer), combine the condensed milk, evaporated milk, whole milk, and Nutella and mix on low speed (be careful, it will splash) until smooth, about 2 minutes. Set aside.

Once the cake has cooled, use a fork to poke holes all over the top of the cake. Working in batches, pour the Nutella mixture slowly and evenly over the top of the cake until the liquid has absorbed. Make sure that each addition of liquid absorbs well into the cake before adding more, and poke more holes, if needed, to prevent overflow of the liquid.

Make the whipped cream topping:
In the bowl of a stand mixer fitted with the whisk attachment (or in a large glass or metal bowl using a handheld mixer), combine the heavy cream, cocoa powder, and sugar and whisk on medium speed until soft peaks form, about 4 minutes.

Evenly spoon the whipped cream onto the top of the cake and gently spread it into an even layer. Refrigerate the cake, uncovered, for at least 2 hours before serving.

Drizzle the whole cake with warm Nutella and sprinkle the crushed cookies over the top. Cut into squares and serve. Refrigerate any leftovers, covered, for up to 2 days.

LEMON BLUEBERRY LOAF CAKE

Serves 6

Total time: 1 hour 15 minutes, plus 30 minutes cooling time

This was the first cake I ever baked and the first video I filmed, so it's near and dear to me. Amazingly, you all seemed to agree, since my video went viral with 18.9 million views! I still can't believe it. It changed my life! This simple cake is tender, moist, and bursting with blueberries. Drizzled with a lemony sugar glaze but not too sweet, this is one of Izzy's and my favorite after-school snacks, and it's also perfect to nibble on at Saturday brunch.

Baking spray, for the pan

1½ cups plus 3 tablespoons all-purpose flour

1½ teaspoons baking powder

½ teaspoon salt

8 tablespoons (1 stick) unsalted butter, at room temperature

¾ cup granulated sugar

Grated zest of 1 lemon

2 large eggs

1 teaspoon vanilla extract

1 cup frozen blueberries

½ cup whole or 2% milk

¼ cup powdered sugar

2 tablespoons fresh lemon juice

COCINA TIP:

• Tossing the blueberries with flour ensures they will not sink to the bottom of the batter.

Preheat the oven to 350°F. Grease a 9 x 5-inch loaf pan with baking spray.

In a medium bowl, whisk together 1½ cups of the flour, the baking powder, and the salt. Set aside.

In the bowl of a stand mixer fitted with the paddle attachment (or in a large glass or metal bowl using a handheld mixer), beat the butter on medium speed until soft and creamy, about 1 minute. Add the granulated sugar and lemon zest and mix until fluffy, about 1 minute. Add the eggs, one at a time, beating well after each addition. Add the vanilla and mix until smooth, 30 seconds to 1 minute.

Reduce the mixer speed to low and slowly pulse in the flour mixture in two batches, mixing until no streaks of flour remain, about 30 seconds. Slowly add the milk and mix until just combined, about 45 seconds.

In a small bowl, toss the blueberries with the remaining 3 tablespoons flour (see Tip) and mix until evenly coated. Using a rubber spatula, gently fold the berries into the batter. Transfer the batter to the prepared loaf pan.

Bake until golden brown and a toothpick inserted into the center comes out clean, about 55 minutes. Let cool completely in the pan on a wire rack, at least 30 minutes.

Right before serving, in a small bowl, stir the powdered sugar and lemon juice until evenly combined.

To assemble:
After the loaf has cooled, run a knife around the edges of the pan and carefully flip the cake out onto the rack. Right before serving, set a baking sheet or aluminum foil under the rack and pour the lemon glaze over the cake.

Transfer to a serving dish, cut yourself a slice, and enjoy!

NO-BAKE LIME CHEESECAKE

Serves 8

Total time: 20 minutes, plus 4 hours refrigeration time

Believe it or not, I had never heard of this traditional Mexican dessert until last year! I don't know what took me so long, but now I'm obsessed! It's tart, sweet, and a fast solution when you're busy or it's too hot outside to turn on the oven. Of course, as with so many things, I think these are even better with a sprinkle of crushed Marias Gamesa cookies. If you can't find them, substitute vanilla wafers.

Baking spray, for the pie plate

1 (14-ounce) can sweetened condensed milk

1 (12-ounce) can evaporated milk

8 ounces cream cheese, at room temperature

½ cup fresh lime juice

1½ (4.9-ounce) packages Marias Gamesa cookies

Thinly sliced lime rounds, for garnish

Coat a 9-inch pie plate with baking spray.

In a blender, combine the condensed milk, evaporated milk, cream cheese, and lime juice and blend on high until smooth, about 3 minutes.

Place 10 of the cookies in a resealable bag and use a rolling pin to crush them into coarse pieces. Set the crushed cookies aside.

Layer one-quarter of the remaining whole cookies over the bottom of the pie plate. Pour one-quarter of the cream cheese mixture on top of the cookie layer and use an offset spatula to spread the mixture to evenly cover the cookie layer. Repeat this process, ending with the cheese mixture, until the pie plate is filled.

Sprinkle the reserved crushed cookies on top of the final cream cheese layer and garnish with lime slices.

Cover and refrigerate for at least 4 hours, or until set, before serving.

Slice the cake and serve immediately on individual plates.

MEXICAN TIRAMISU

Serves 8

Total time: 40 minutes, plus overnight chilling

Cooking shows inspire me, and as I was watching someone make tiramisu, I wondered if the dessert would be even better if you replaced the ladyfingers with my favorite Mexican Marias Gamesa cookies, which are similar to vanilla wafers. The result was this Mexican-Italian mash-up! It's an irresistible, crowd-pleasing recipe made more manageable because it must be made a day in advance, leaving you with one less thing to do on a party day.

Room-temperature butter, for greasing

6 large egg yolks

¾ cup granulated sugar

8 ounces mascarpone cheese

2 teaspoons vanilla extract

2 cups heavy cream

1 cup brewed coffee (decaf or regular), at room temperature

1 (19.7-ounce) package Marias Gamesa cookies (see Tip)

¼ cup unsweetened cocoa powder

Lightly grease a 9 x 9-inch baking pan with butter.

In a heatproof bowl that can fit over a small pot of boiling water, combine the egg yolks and sugar. Bring 1 cup water to a boil in the pot over high heat. Reduce the heat to low, and set the bowl on top (make sure the bowl doesn't touch the water). Cook, whisking constantly, until the egg yolks turn pale yellow and the sugar has dissolved, about 5 minutes. Remove the bowl from the pot, and let cool to room temperature.

In a large bowl using a rubber spatula, fold together the mascarpone and vanilla until combined. Gently fold in the egg yolk mixture until everything is well incorporated.

In the bowl of a stand mixer fitted with the whisk attachment (or in a large glass or metal bowl using a handheld mixer), beat the heavy cream until it forms soft peaks, about 5 minutes. Using a spatula, fold the egg yolk mixture into the whipped cream.

To assemble:
Pour the coffee into a shallow bowl. Dip the cookies into the coffee one at a time until coated, and line them up in the greased baking dish until the bottom is covered. Evenly spread a 1-inch-thick layer of the whipped cream mixture over the cookies. Repeat with the cookies dipped in coffee and the cream until the baking dish is filled, ending with the cream. Using a sieve, dust the top layer of cream with the cocoa powder. Cover with plastic wrap and refrigerate.

Evenly divide the tiramisu among eight dessert bowls or large glasses and serve.

COCINA TIP:

• If you can't find Marias Gamesa cookies, use the standard ladyfingers.

BREAD PUDDING

Anytime I have leftover bolillo bread or any other bread or rolls, this luscious, super-easy raisin caramel pudding sold at Mexican *panaderias* (bakeries) always comes to mind! This is one time when stale bread is really what you want, so it can soak up the sweet custard while still keeping a little of its shape and texture. Now there's no need to visit a Mexican *panaderia*.

Room-temperature unsalted butter, for greasing

5 stale bolillos or kaiser rolls, cut into 1-inch chunks (about 5 cups)

3 cups whole milk

3 large eggs, beaten

1½ cups granulated sugar

½ cup dark or golden raisins

4 tablespoons (½ stick) unsalted butter, melted

1½ teaspoons ground cinnamon

1½ teaspoons vanilla extract

Preheat the oven to 350°F. Lightly grease the bottom and sides of a 9 x 9-inch baking pan with 2-inch-tall sides (see Tips).

In a large bowl, combine the bread cubes and milk and use a spatula or wooden spoon to mix until the bread has soaked up the milk. Add the eggs, ½ cup of the sugar, the raisins, melted butter, cinnamon, and vanilla and mix until well combined. Set aside.

Heat a large skillet over medium heat. Add the remaining 1 cup sugar and cook, whisking constantly to prevent it from burning, until it melts and turns a light brown, about 8 minutes. The sugar will melt slowly at first and then very quickly, so be patient and keep your eye on the pan. Carefully, pour the melted sugar into the prepared baking pan, using a silicone spatula to spread it out to the edges, covering the bottom of the pan.

Pour the bread batter on top of the sugar, spreading it out the edges, too. Place the baking dish into a larger 18 x 13-inch baking dish and place on a pulled-out oven rack. Carefully pour in enough warm water into the larger baking dish to come three-quarters of the way up the sides of the baking pan with the bread pudding.

Bake until golden brown on top and a knife inserted into the center comes out clean, about 1 hour. Let cool on a wire rack for about 10 minutes.

Slice the cake while it's warm so the caramel is still soft and serve on individual plates.

COCINA TIPS:

- Do not use a ceramic baking dish for this recipe. Ceramic material is sensitive to heat fluctuations, and pouring the melted sugar into a ceramic dish could cause it to shatter or crack.

- Hot sugar is dangerous, so be extra careful when making caramel! I always have a bowl of ice water standing by in case of burns.

- Be patient and don't take your eyes off the sugar. It will take a while to melt, but once it starts, it will begin to brown and turn dark very quickly, and can go from brown to burnt in a matter of seconds.

- Make sure you use a heatproof silicone spoon or spatula to stir the sugar. The last thing you need is for bits of rubber or plastic to melt into your caramel!

RICE PUDDING

Serves 8 to 10

Total time: 1 hour, plus 15 minutes or up to overnight cooling time

My mom could never quite get her rice pudding recipe right, so I spent a lot of time tinkering with it, hoping to perfect it for the family, and I think I nailed it. I prefer it slightly less sweet than my husband and Izzy, but I've deferred to them here and included the maximum amount of sugar. It's a very forgiving recipe, so play around with the amounts and try it with a little less sugar—then reach out and let me know if you're on Team Edith!

2 cups uncooked extra-long-grain white rice (I prefer Mahatma), thoroughly rinsed and drained (see Tips)

½ cup granulated sugar, or ⅓ cup you prefer it to be less sweet

2 cinnamon sticks

¼ teaspoon salt

6 cups whole milk

1 (14-ounce) can sweetened condensed milk

1 (12-ounce) can evaporated milk

Ground cinnamon, for garnish

Handful of dark or golden raisins, for garnish

In a large lidded pot, bring 4 cups water to a boil over high heat. Add the rice, sugar, cinnamon sticks, and salt. Reduce the heat to medium-low, cover, and simmer for 20 minutes.

Add the whole milk, condensed milk, and evaporated milk and use a spatula or wooden spoon to mix until combined. Cover and cook, stirring occasionally to make sure the rice isn't sticking to the pot, until the rice is fully cooked, 25 minutes. The pudding should still look runny, but this is okay (see Tips).

Transfer the rice pudding to a serving dish and sprinkle with cinnamon and the raisins. Let cool at room temperature for at least 15 minutes before serving, or refrigerate and serve cold.

COCINA TIPS:

• To rinse rice, place it in a fine-mesh sieve and rinse under cool running water until the water runs clear, about 2 minutes. Shake to drain well.

• The pudding will thicken significantly as it cools, so don't worry if it still looks very loose and milky after cooking.

BUÑUELOS

Serves 4 to 6 (makes 10 buñuelos)

Total time: 25 minutes, plus 30 minutes resting time

Typically, buñuelos are a traditional treat made around Christmas and New Year's. But we like to indulge in them all winter, especially with a cup of Chocolate Caliente Mexicano (page 203), which brings the warm-inside feeling from the classic cinnamon-sugar mix. My version is more like a fried tortilla than a typical donut, which I think makes them extra special.

4 cups all-purpose flour, plus more for dusting

4¼ cups canola or other neutral oil

1½ teaspoons baking powder

½ teaspoon salt

1 teaspoon vanilla extract

1½ cups granulated sugar

1½ tablespoons ground cinnamon

In a large bowl, combine the flour, ¼ cup of the oil, the baking powder, salt, and vanilla. Add ½ cup warm water and, using your hands, mix until the water is absorbed. Add more water, 1 tablespoon at a time, until the dough comes together and is stretchy like pizza dough.

Remove the dough from the bowl and knead on a lightly floured counter until smooth and elastic, about 3 minutes. Return the dough to the bowl, cover with a clean kitchen towel, and allow to rest in a warm spot for 30 minutes.

Divide the dough into 10 equal portions (about 2 ounces each) and roll into balls. Using a rolling pin, roll each ball on a lightly floured surface until they are flat and thin and about 6 inches in diameter.

Mix the sugar and cinnamon in a large baking dish. Set aside.

Heat the remaining 4 cups oil in a Dutch oven or a deep heavy pot over medium heat until it

reaches 350°F on a deep-fry thermometer. (If you don't have a deep-fry thermometer, dip a wooden toothpick in the oil; if the oil bubbles, it's ready.)

Working with one dough round at a time, add to the hot oil and cook until golden brown, about 1 minute. Using tongs, flip and cook until crispy and brown all over, about 30 seconds more. Immediately transfer the buñuelo to the sugar/cinnamon mixture and turn to coat each side.

Transfer to serving plate and serve immediately, or at room temperature.

COCINA TIPS:

- These can be made in advance and served at room temperature.

- You'll want to use tongs to press down on the buñuelos as they fry to prevent large air pockets from forming.

CHURROS

Serves 6 to 8 (makes 20 churros)

Total time: 30 minutes

Churros are another classic Mexican street food, sold from carts to kids of all ages. We always eat these at Disneyland, and I played with the recipe so we could fry them up at home. They are similar to buñuelos (page 198) but deliciously different because of the type of dough and their shape. More of a cream puff dough, these churros are piped in little 4-inch logs right into hot oil, then fried until golden brown and crispy and rolled in cinnamon sugar. It takes practice to get the piping technique down, so be patient, but even the imperfect ones taste delicious! And if you're up for a little extra challenge, you can use a piping bag to fill them up with Nutella once slightly cooled.

Dough:
8 tablespoons (1 stick) salted butter, at room temperature
½ cup whole milk
¼ teaspoon salt
1¾ cups all-purpose flour
½ teaspoon vanilla extract
¼ teaspoon ground cinnamon
3 large eggs
4 cups of canola or other neutral oil, for deep-frying

Cinnamon Sugar:
½ cup granulated sugar
1 teaspoon ground cinnamon

Make the dough:
In a medium saucepan, combine the butter, milk, ½ cup water, and salt. Heat over medium heat until the butter has melted and is bubbling, about 3 minutes. Add the flour and stir with a wooden spoon until the dough becomes a thick ball with a soft consistency, 1 to 2 minutes.

Transfer the dough into a stand mixer fitted with the paddle (or in a large glass or metal bowl using a hand mixer). Mixing on low speed, add the vanilla and cinnamon and beat until smooth, about 10 seconds. Add the eggs one at a time, beating well after each addition, and beat until fully incorporated, about 1 minute.

Continue mixing for about 2 more minutes, or until the dough is smooth, soft, and stretchy and begins to pull away from the sides of the bowl.

Transfer the dough to a piping bag fitted with a ½-inch tip (or a freezer bag with ½ inch cut off of one corner).

Set a wire rack in a baking sheet and have it near the stove. Heat the oil in a Dutch oven over medium heat until it reaches 350°F on a deep-fry thermometer. (If you don't have a deep-fry thermometer, test the oil by squeezing in a small bit of the dough; if the oil sizzles and the dough floats to the top, the oil is ready for frying.)

RECIPE CONTINUES

Working in batches of about 4 churros to avoid crowding the pan, carefully squeeze the dough from the piping bag into the hot oil, using scissors to snip the end of the churros into the oil to form 4-inch lengths. Fry until golden brown on one side, about 1 minute. Using tongs, flip the churros and fry until golden brown on the other side, about 1 minute more. Transfer the churros to the rack to cool and repeat with the remaining dough.

Make the cinnamon sugar:
In a large bowl, whisk together the sugar and cinnamon until combined.

When the churros are cool enough to handle, using tongs, toss them in the bowl with the cinnamon-sugar mixture until coated.

Transfer to a serving plate and serve immediately.

COCINA TIPS:

- Forming churros takes practice, so don't worry if yours are a bit funny-looking. They will still be delicious!

- We are always happy to eat these with ice cream and sliced strawberries.

CHOCOLATE CALIENTE MEXICANO

Serves 4   *Total time: 10 minutes*

Izzy and I like nothing better than to snuggle on the couch with our favorite movie and stir our hot chocolate with cinnamon sticks. The Mexican accent comes courtesy of the cinnamon in the Mexican chocolate tablets (and, of course, the cinnamon sticks). These are just the thing to pair with my Conchas (page 44).

4 cups whole milk

½ cup heavy cream

1 Mexican chocolate tablet, preferably Ibarra

2 cinnamon sticks

Pinch of salt

In a small pot, combine the milk, heavy cream, chocolate, cinnamon sticks, and salt. Cook over medium-high heat, stirring constantly (see Tip), until the chocolate has fully melted, about 3 minutes. Skim off any milk skin from the top.

Pour into four mugs and enjoy!

COCINA TIP:

• Traditionally, this is made with a molinillo, a beautifully carved wooden "frother." Use it the same way you would a whisk. You can also use a milk frother, but it's not as much fun!

SWEET CHEESE QUESADILLA

Serves 6

Total time: 1 hour

My husband, Brandon, has a blend of Mexican and Salvadoran heritage, and this recipe comes from his great-aunt's treasured collection. At a family gathering on one of our early dates, Brandon offered me a "quesadilla." Expecting the typical griddled, cheese-filled tortillas, I was taken aback when he handed me a piece of his great-aunt's sweet, cheesy, rich cornbread. We shared a good laugh over the mix-up, but it was a delightful introduction to his family's traditions and recipes, which have now become a cherished part of our own.

Baking spray, for the pan

2 cups rice flour

1 tablespoon baking powder

1 cup granulated sugar

4 tablespoons (½ stick) unsalted butter, at room temperature

2 large eggs

1 cup grated Cotija cheese

½ cup crema Salvadoreña or Mexican crema (see Tip)

½ cup whole milk

1 tablespoon vanilla extract

1 tablespoon sesame seeds

Preheat the oven to 350°F. Lightly grease a 9 x 13-inch baking pan with baking spray.

In a small bowl, whisk together the rice flour and baking powder until evenly combined. Set aside.

In the bowl of a stand mixer fitted with the paddle attachment (or in a large glass or metal bowl using a handheld mixer), beat the sugar and butter on medium speed until creamy, about 2 minutes. Add the eggs one at a time, beating well after each addition, 1 to 2 minutes.

Reduce the mixer speed to low and beat in the Cotija until just combined, about 30 seconds.

Add 1 cup of the rice flour mixture and mix until just combined, 25 to 45 seconds. Add the crema, milk, and vanilla and mix until combined, 30 seconds to 1 minute. Add the remaining rice flour mixture and mix until the flour is completely incorporated, about 30 seconds. Transfer the batter to the prepared baking pan and sprinkle with the sesame seeds.

Bake for 30 to 40 minutes, until a toothpick inserted into the center comes out clean.

Cool for 30 minutes and cut into large squares and enjoy!

COCINA TIP:

- If you can't find crema Salvadoreña or crema Mexicana, thin the same amount of sour cream with a little milk.

FRESAS CON CREMA

Serves 6

Total time: 20 minutes, plus 2 hours refrigeration time

This is not your typical whipped heavy cream and berries! My Mexican version ups the game with a blend of condensed milk, media crema, sour cream, and a hint of vanilla, resulting in a sweet, rich dessert with a bit of tang from the sour cream. This is the dessert I dream of on hot summer days.

1 (14-ounce) can sweetened condensed milk

1 (7.6-ounce) can media crema, or 1 cup evaporated milk

3 tablespoons sour cream

2 teaspoons vanilla extract

1 pound strawberries, hulled and thinly sliced, plus more for garnish

In a large bowl, combine the condensed milk, media crema, sour cream, and vanilla and beat with a handheld mixer or a whisk until smooth and fluffy. Add the strawberries and gently fold to combine. Cover and refrigerate for at least 2 hours.

Evenly spoon the chilled mixture into individual dessert bowls or a large serving bowl, garnish with more strawberries, and serve immediately.

DEVILISHLY DELICIOUS ICE POPS

Serves 8

Total time: 15 minutes, plus 6 hours freezing time

We call these *diablitos*, or "little devils," because it's truly sinful how delicious they taste! During our summers in Mexico, there was a sweet older woman who sold her handmade cones across the street from my grandpa's mini-mart. I created this recipe for Izzy, my sweet little devil. Made with frozen mango juice mixed with Tajín spice and chamoy (a pickled dried fruit and lime condiment), these rival the ices I had as a kid.

3 large mangoes, diced

2 tablespoons granulated sugar

¼ cup chamoy, plus more for garnish

2 teaspoons Tajín, plus more for garnish

8 ice pop sticks

Set eight 9-ounce freezer-safe glasses on a tray or baking pan that will fit in your freezer.

In a blender, combine the mangoes, sugar, and 2 cups water and blend on high until creamy, about 45 seconds.

Spoon the chamoy and Tajín into the glasses, dividing them evenly. Top with the blended mango. Place the glasses in the freezer for 30 minutes to firm up. Remove from the freezer, place an ice pop stick in the center of each glass, and return them to the freezer for 6 hours or until fully frozen.

Fill a large bowl with warm water. Dip each glass into the water to separate the glass from the diablito. Sprinkle the top of each diablito with more Tajín and/or chamoy for garnish.

Place the diablitos on a platter or hand them to hungry little devils immediately!

PALETAS DE FRESAS

Serves 12

Total time: 5 minutes, plus 4 hours freezing time

Everyone remembers eating ice pops growing up. These strawberry *paletas* (popsicles)—made with fresh strawberries—deliver on all that nostalgia and are so much better for you than many store-bought versions. Whenever I come across a perfect batch of strawberries, I buy extra and freeze them for these.

2 pounds strawberries, hulled or frozen

1 cup granulated sugar

1½ tablespoons fresh lime juice

In a blender, combine the strawberries, sugar, lime juice, and 2 cups water and blend on high until smooth and creamy, 1 to 2 minutes. Evenly divide the mixture among twelve ice pop molds. Place the molds in the freezer for 30 minutes to firm up. Remove from the freezer, place an ice pop stick in the center of each mold, and return them to the freezer for at least 4 hours or until fully frozen.

Dip the molds into warm water for 5 seconds or as long as needed to loosen the ice pops from the molds. Unmold and serve immediately.

COCINA TIP:

- If you have any of the strawberry mixture left over after filling the molds, enjoy it as a smoothie!

CUCUMBER, LIME, AND CHIA SMOOTHIE

Serves 6 to 8   *Total time: 20 minutes*

This is one of the most popular Mexican summer drinks, although we love it year-round. *Pepinos* (cucumbers) are so refreshing, especially when accented with lime and sweetened with sugar. The chia seeds add a fun texture and are a terrific source of fiber, too. I wouldn't say no to this with a little tequila blanco, either!

3 large cucumbers, peeled and diced (about 6 cups)

1 cup fresh lime juice (from 6 to 8 limes)

1 cup granulated sugar, plus more as needed

5 tablespoons chia seeds

Lime slices, for garnish

In a blender, combine the cucumbers, lime juice, and sugar and blend on high until smooth. Transfer to a 1-gallon container or large bowl. Add 5 cups water and the chia seeds and mix until well combined. Taste and add more sugar, if desired.

Pour the mixture into a large pitcher and stir in 2 to 3 cups of ice. Or, pour it into individual glasses filled with ice. Float the lime slices in the pitcher or garnish the glasses with lime slices and serve immediately.

HIBISCUS COOLER

Serves 6 to 8

Total time: 30 minutes, plus 1 hour refrigeration time

Dried jamaica (hibiscus) flowers lend a lovely red color and a light, sweet, floral tartness to many tea blends. In Mexico, you'll find them in sauces, marinades, and this very popular drink, sweetened with sugar and a bit of lime. You'll always find a pitcher in my fridge, and it's great for gatherings.

2 cups dried jamaica (hibiscus) flowers
1 cup granulated sugar
1 tablespoon fresh lime juice

In a large pot, combine 6 cups water, the jamaica flowers, and sugar. Bring to a boil over high heat, then reduce the heat to low and simmer until the sugar has dissolved, about 20 minutes. Remove from the heat and pour in 4 cups cold water. Strain the liquid through a fine-mesh sieve into a large pitcher (discard the flowers). Let cool for at least 1 hour.

Stir in the lime juice and 2 cups ice and serve immediately.

COCINA TIP:

- To this make in advance, stir in the lime juice and refrigerate until ready to serve, then add the ice just before serving.

HORCHATA

Serves 6

Total time: 15 minutes, plus 4 hours soaking time

Commonly sold on the streets of Mexico, this refreshing and creamy drink is ideal when served alongside a spicy taco, but I think it's an excellent choice for any meal or even by itself. The base is made with rice that's been soaked on the counter overnight, then mixed with milk and spices and blended. I hope you'll whip up a batch of this for your family—it's fun to see if they can guess that there's rice in their shake!

1½ cups uncooked long-grain rice, thoroughly rinsed and drained (see Tip)

1 cinnamon stick

1 whole clove

½ cup granulated sugar

5 cups whole milk

1 (14-ounce) can sweetened condensed milk

1 (12-ounce) can evaporated milk

1½ tablespoons vanilla extract

Ground cinnamon, for garnish

In a large container with a lid or a large bowl, combine the rice, cinnamon stick, clove, and 4 cups water. Cover and soak in the refrigerator for 4 hours or up to overnight.

Transfer the rice mixture to a blender, add the sugar, and blend on high until the rice and spices are thoroughly broken down and the mixture is well combined, about 1 minute. Taste and add more sugar, if desired.

Strain the mixture through a fine-mesh sieve or cheesecloth set over a large bowl. Discard the solids. Stir in the whole milk, condensed milk, evaporated milk, and vanilla. If the mixture is too thick stir in up to 2 cups water to thin it out.

Pour into glasses (over ice, if desired), garnish with ground cinnamon, and serve immediately.

COCINA TIP:

- To rinse rice, place it in a fine-mesh sieve and rinse under cool running water until the water runs clear, about 2 minutes. Shake to drain well.

CHOCOLATE AND CORN PUDDING

Serves 6 to 8

Total time: 25 minutes

My mom used to make massive batches of this chocolate atole pudding all winter because there's no better way to warm yourself on a chilly night. Now I do the same for my family and friends. The pudding is very aromatic, rich, and creamy, thanks to blending whole cloves and cinnamon sticks with masa harina (Mexican corn flour),, three types of milk, and chocolate. I love using Mexican piloncillo, but dark brown sugar is an easy swap. Morning, afternoon, or evening, there's never a wrong time of day to savor this!

1 cup masa harina (instant white corn flour), preferably Maseca

1 cup (8 ounces) grated piloncillo or dark brown sugar

2 cinnamon sticks

7 whole cloves

1 cup roughly chopped Mexican chocolate tablets, preferably Ibarra (2 tablets)

6 cups whole milk

1 (14-ounce) can sweetened condensed milk

1 (12-ounce) can evaporated milk

1 tablespoon vanilla extract

In a small dry saucepan, toast the corn flour over medium-low heat, stirring occasionally to prevent burning, until lightly browned, about 5 minutes. Transfer the toasted masa flour to a plate and set aside to cool slightly.

In a 4-quart pot, bring 4 cups water to a boil over medium-low heat. Stir in the piloncillo, cinnamon sticks, cloves, and chocolate and cook, stirring constantly until the piloncillo has dissolved completely, about 1 minute.

In a blender, combine the whole milk, condensed milk, evaporated milk, vanilla, and toasted corn flour and blend on high until combined, about 45 seconds.

While whisking constantly, slowly pour the blended milk mixture into the pot with the melted chocolate. Cook, whisking constantly, until the flour is well incorporated, the liquid has thickened slightly, and the atole de chocolate is warmed through, about 5 minutes.

Pour into individual mugs and serve warm.

COCINA TIP:

- This makes a big batch, but you can refrigerate leftovers in an airtight container for up to 1 week. Reheat on the stove or in the microwave; you may need to stir in a little more milk when reheating.

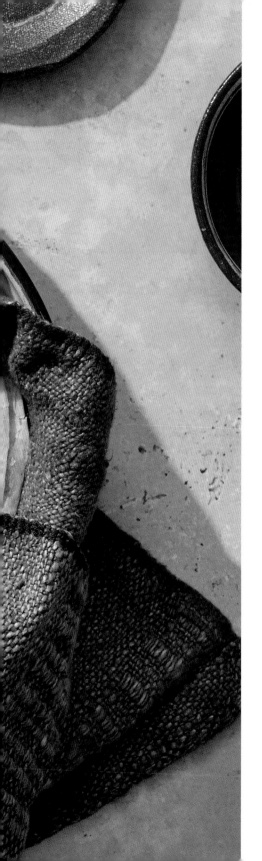

BASICS

CORN TORTILLAS

Makes 10 (6-inch) tortillas   *Total time: 20 minutes*

Corn tortillas date back to prehistoric times—preceding flour tortillas, even—and are a staple in North American and Mexican cultures. Growing up, my mom would have me help her make the *masa* (dough) for them, and it always took me a while to find the right texture. But with some practice, I got the hang of it, and now it's second nature. I prefer using a classic wooden tortilla press, just like my grandmother (see Tips). I like to sprinkle a little salt on my tortillas and roll them up, and I think they're perfect just like that. Like my Flour Tortillas (page 224), these are used in so many recipes in the book, but are great simply cut into wedges and fried for chips.

2 cups masa harina (instant corn masa flour), preferably Maseca

2 teaspoons salt

1½ cups room-temperature water, plus more if needed

Line a baking sheet with plastic wrap or parchment paper.

In a large bowl, whisk together the masa flour and salt until combined. While mixing constantly with your hands, gradually add the warm water, until a dough forms. Continue to mix until the dough no longer sticks to your hands.

Line a tortilla press on both sides with plastic wrap so the dough won't stick. Divide the dough into 10 equal pieces (about 2 tablespoons each) and roll them into balls the size of golf balls. Place one ball of dough on the tortilla press, close the press, and press down to flatten the dough into a tortilla. Open the tortilla press and remove the tortilla, still on the bottom piece of plastic. Place the tortilla on a baking sheet. Line the bottom of the tortilla press with a new piece of plastic wrap and repeat with the remaining dough balls.

Set out a tortilla warmer (or line a large bowl with a large kitchen towel) and have it near the stove. Heat a comal, griddle, or large dry skillet over high heat. Working in batches, place as many tortillas as will fit at one time on the pan. Cook until the tortillas begin to puff up and develop golden brown spots on one side, about 1½ minutes. Flip and cook until golden brown spots develop on the other side, about 1 minute more. Transfer to the tortilla warmer to keep warm and repeat with the remaining tortillas.

COCINA TIPS:

- A tortilla press is usually made of cast-iron, cast-aluminum, or good old-fashioned wood—which I prefer. It's a tool designed to flatten balls of dough into evenly round tortillas, saving you lots of effort and time instead of rolling.

- If you don't have a tortilla press, you can use the bottom of a plate. Place a piece of plastic wrap over both sides of the dough, then press down with the plate and flatten the dough into a ¼-inch-thick round.

- Tortillas can dry out quickly, and a tortilla warmer will keep them soft, supple, and ready throughout the meal. Pick up the woven wicker type, round and perfectly sized to fit corn tortillas, at a local Mexican grocery store or online.

- Store leftover tortillas in a large resealable plastic bag in the refrigerator for up to 1 week. Reheat on the stovetop using the comal, griddle, or dry skillet for about 30 seconds per side, or wrap in a kitchen or paper towel and microwave in 15-second intervals until warm. A large stack takes about 45 seconds.

FLOUR TORTILLAS

Makes 20 (6-inch) tortillas

Total time: 30 minutes, plus resting time

There's no comparison between store-bought flour tortillas and homemade. They're like an entirely different food. Slathered with butter, they are my weakness. And despite what you may think, they're simple to make yourself. They're so soft and thin, they practically melt into any filling stuffed inside. If you can find lard, please try it. Lard is actually lower in saturated fat and cholesterol than butter, and it makes for the most delicate, flavorful tortillas. They're such a foundational element in Mexican cuisine that these homemade tortillas work with almost every recipe in this book, but try them in my Fried Quesadillas (page 96).

7 cups all-purpose flour, cut into tablespoons, plus more as needed

1 tablespoon salt

1 cup lard, or 1 cup (2 sticks) cold unsalted butter, plus more for greasing

2 cups warm water, or more as needed

In a large bowl, whisk together the flour and salt. Add the lard (or butter) and, using your fingertips, rub it into the flour until the mixture is sandy and holds together when squeezed with your hands. Slowly drizzle in the warm water and use your hands to mix until you have a soft, cohesive dough that is stretchy like pizza dough. If the dough still has not come together, add more water, 1 tablespoon at a time; if the dough seems too wet, add more flour, ¼ cup at a time.

Turn the dough out onto a lightly floured surface and knead until smooth, about 4 minutes. Shape the dough into a ball. Wipe out the bowl you used to make the dough, grease it with some lard, and return the dough to the bowl. Lightly coat the top of the dough with a light layer of lard. Cover with a kitchen towel and let rest in a warm spot for 20 minutes.

Divide the dough into 20 equal portions (about 2½ ounces each). Roll each portion into a ball and use a rolling pin to roll each ball into a 6-inch round (about ¼ inch thick).

Set out a tortilla warmer (or line a large bowl with a large kitchen towel) and have it near the stove. Heat a comal, nonstick griddle, or large dry cast-iron skillet over medium heat. Cook one tortilla at a time until they fluff up, about 2 minutes. Flip and cook on the other side until puffy, about 1 minute more. The tortillas should have beautiful brown charred spots on both sides. Transfer to the tortilla warmer to keep warm and repeat with the remaining tortillas.

COCINA TIP:

- If you are new to rolling tortillas, be patient. It takes a little practice.

SALSA ROJA

Makes 1½ cups *Total time: 20 minutes*

This salsa gets its rich red hue from dried guajillo and de árbol chiles, blended with garlic and salt—an ideal companion for dipping chips. We also love to pour a few spoonfuls on our Flautas (page 127) and Sopes de Soy Chorizo (page 130) or any of the tacos in the book.

5 dried guajillo chiles, stemmed, split, and seeded

3 dried chiles de árbol, whole

10 tomatillos, husked and rinsed (see Tips)

3 garlic cloves, peeled but whole

3 teaspoons salt

Heat a comal or large pan over low to medium heat and roast then combine the guajillo chiles and chiles de árbol, pressing the guajillo chiles with a spatula to flatten them. Cook the chiles 1 to 2 minutes per side. Roasting longer than 2 minutes will make the chiles bitter.

Fill a large bowl with warm water and add the chiles.

Cook the tomatillos on the comal until they are lightly charred, about 2 minutes per side. Set aside to cool slightly.

Drain the chiles and add them to a blender with the tomatillos, garlic, salt, and ½ cup water. With the steam vent in the blender top open, pulse until smooth, about 10 pulses. The mixture should have the texture of tomato sauce. If it's too thick, add up to ½ cup more water and blend until smooth, about 20 seconds.

To serve, transfer the salsa to a bowl and serve with tortilla chips.

COCINA TIPS:

- To clean tomatillos, first remove the outer husk, then thoroughly clean with cool water and fruit and veggie wash or natural dish soap to remove the sticky residue.

- If not using immediately, allow the salsa to cool, then transfer to a jar or other airtight container and refrigerate for up to 5 days or freeze up to 2 months.

CHIPOTLE SALSA

Makes 1 cup   *Total time: 10 minutes*

The fire of the chipotles (smoked jalapeños) in adobo gets tamed—just a bit—by creamy yogurt and a tart squeeze of lemon in this smoky sauce. Pair it with Tacos de Camarones (page 86) or drizzle it over grilled meat, fish, or veggies for a fast and flavorful dish. Since this recipe yields a small amount, I prefer to make this with an immersion blender; a mini food processor works, too.

1 cup plain nonfat yogurt

2 canned chipotle peppers in adobo sauce

1 garlic clove, peeled but whole

2 tablespoons finely chopped fresh parsley

½ teaspoon salt

½ teaspoon ground black pepper

Juice of ½ lemon

Combine all the ingredients in an immersion blender cup, blender, or food processor and blend on high until smooth, about 1 minute. Use immediately or transfer the salsa to a jar or other airtight container and refrigerate for up to 4 days.

COCINA TIP:

- This is one of the only times I use an immersion blender. It makes a smooth sauce and is easy to clean.

CHILE DE ÁRBOL SALSA

Makes about 2 cups

Total time: 10 minutes

Fire alert! The small chile de árbol is mighty in heat and addictive when blended into a salsa. Trust me, once you try it, I guarantee you'll always want to keep some around. It goes with everything, but we can't get enough of it with Tostadas de Tinga (page 116), Tacos de Camarones (page 86), Sopes de Soy Chorizo (page 130), or enchiladas (pages 91 and 92).

¼ cup canola or other neutral oil

12 dried chiles de árbol, stemmed, split, and seeded

4 ripe Roma (plum) tomatoes, roughly chopped

¼ small white onion, peeled and roughly chopped (about ¼ cup)

3 garlic cloves, peeled but whole

1 teaspoon salt

1 teaspoon ground black pepper

½ teaspoon dried oregano

Heat the oil in a small saucepan over medium heat. Add the chiles, tomatoes, onion, and garlic and cook, stirring occasionally, until the onion is translucent and softened, about 7 minutes.

Transfer to a blender and add the salt, black pepper, oregano, and 1 cup water. With the steam vent in the blender top open, blend until smooth, about 30 seconds. Use immediately or transfer the salsa to a jar or other airtight container and refrigerate for up to 1 week.

SALSA FRESCA

Makes 2 cups　　　　　　　　*Total time: 10 minutes*

Salsa fresca is a refreshing mix of veggies (in the red, green, and white colors of Mexico's flag, of course), and many of the dishes in this book would be lost without it. Spiked with lime, it brings a jolt of freshness to tacos, salad or rice bowls, and tortilla chips on game day.

6 ripe Roma (plum) tomatoes, roughly chopped

1 (14.5-ounce) can crushed tomatoes

2 cups fresh cilantro leaves with 2-inch stems

½ small white onion, peeled

4 fresh serrano chiles

3 garlic cloves, peeled but whole

Juice of 1 lime

1 teaspoon salt

Ground black pepper

In a food processor, combine the Roma tomatoes, crushed tomatoes, cilantro, onion, chiles, garlic, lime juice, salt, and black pepper to taste. Pulse for a few seconds until everything is incorporated but the mixture is still chunky. Use immediately or transfer the salsa to a jar or other airtight container and refrigerate for up to 3 days.

CREAMY AVOCADO SALSA

Makes 2 cups　　　　　　*Total time: 5 minutes*

This is my mom's recipe, and I'm so honored to share it here. Mom would throw everything into the blender, blitz it up, and bingo! She incorporates typical salsa ingredients like serrano chiles, white onion, and garlic, but instead of mixing everything with tomatoes, she uses milk. The final product is a creamier marriage of the two best dips in Mexican culture: guacamole and salsa. Drizzle this hot-yet-cool sauce over Tacos De Camarones (page 86), Carne Asada (page 108), or Arroz Rojo (page 167), or serve it as a dip for chips.

2 large Hass avocados, halved and pitted

1 cup whole milk

2 fresh serrano chiles

¼ small white onion, peeled

1 garlic clove, peeled but whole

1 teaspoon chicken bouillon powder, preferably Knorr

1 teaspoon salt

Juice of 1 lime

Scoop the avocado flesh into a blender. Add the milk, serranos, onion, garlic, bouillon powder, salt, and lime juice. Pulse a few times to break down the ingredients, then blend on high speed until completely smooth, about 30 seconds. Transfer the salsa to a jar or other airtight container and refrigerate for up to 3 days.

COCINA TIP:

- If the salsa is too thick, thin it with more milk.

GUACAMOLE SALSA DUPE

Makes 2 cups

Total time: 15 minutes

I always wondered how this one taco stand had the best guacamole, until one day my friends told me it wasn't guacamole at all, and that the whole time I had been eating a mix of Mexican squash and tomatillos. I was shocked, but also thrilled, because the flavor was so convincingly delicious! Everything is charred and blended to create a smoky and smooth salsa that's creamy with a little kick and so delicious, I don't mind being tricked! Your kids will never know they're eating their veggies! I can't fully savor my Carne Asada (page 108) without this.

2 tablespoons canola or other neutral oil

1 medium Mexican squash or zucchini, halved lengthwise and cut crosswise into ½-inch-thick half-moons

3 tomatillos, husked, rinsed, and halved (see Tip)

¼ small white onion, peeled

2 garlic cloves, peeled but whole

1 fresh jalapeño, stemmed and halved

1½ teaspoons salt

Heat the oil in a large skillet over medium heat. Add the squash, tomatillos, onion, garlic, jalapeño, and salt and cook, stirring frequently, until the tomatillos turn a lighter green color and the squash is just tender and mottled brown, about 12 minutes.

Transfer everything to a blender. With the steam vent in the blender top open, blend on high until smooth, about 45 seconds. Transfer the salsa to a jar or other airtight container and refrigerate for up to 4 days.

COCINA TIP:

- To clean tomatillos, first remove the outer husk, then thoroughly clean with cool water and fruit and veggie wash or natural dish soap to remove the sticky residue.

SALSA VERDE

Makes 2 cups

Total time: 25 minutes

Salsa verde can be used in many Mexican dishes—it's up to your imagination. I think I use this salsa the most. This is my base recipe, and I use variations of it throughout the book. Here I blanch the chiles and tomatillos so the flavor is light and zippy. It's great with chips or my Fried Quesadillas (page 96). Sometimes I char the vegetables to deepen the flavor, as I do for Costillas en Salsa (page 136).

5 fresh jalapeños, or
4 or 5 serrano chiles

½ pound tomatillos (about 9), husked and rinsed (see Tip)

1½ cups roughly chopped fresh cilantro

½ small white onion, peeled and diced (about ⅓ cup)

3 garlic cloves, peeled but whole

1 tablespoon chicken bouillon powder, preferably Knorr

1 teaspoon ground cumin

1 teaspoon dried oregano

In a medium pot, combine the chiles and 4 cups water and bring to a boil over medium heat. Reduce the heat to low and simmer for 4 minutes. Add the tomatillos and cook until they turn a brownish-yellow color, about 5 minutes. Drain the chiles and tomatillos and let cool for 10 minutes.

Transfer the chiles and tomatillos to a blender. Add the cilantro, onion, garlic, bouillon powder, cumin, oregano, and 1 cup water. With the steam vent in the blender top open, blend until smooth, about 45 seconds. Use immediately or transfer the salsa to a jar or other airtight container and refrigerate for up to 3 days.

COCINA TIP:

- To clean tomatillos, first remove the outer husk, then thoroughly clean with cool water and fruit and veggie wash or natural dish soap to remove the sticky residue.

EDITH'S FAVORITE GUACAMOLE

Serves 4

Total time: 10 minutes, plus 2 hours refrigeration time

Avocados are central to Mexican cooking, and guacamole is found on almost any Mexican table or restaurant menu. Guacamole is a love language, and this all-star is the one that tastes like home. This may be controversial, but I'm not a big fan of fresh jalapeños in my guac; I prefer the pickled ones. Growing up, my brothers and I were not fans of white onions, so Mom finely diced red for us instead. The avocados aren't mashed until smooth, but instead left chunky, bringing you more texture and personality. Roughly mixed with tomato, chiles, onion, lime juice, and chopped cilantro, this is the guac for thick tortilla chips, and the one I serve the most as an appetizer.

2 large Hass avocados, halved and pitted

1 cup finely chopped fresh cilantro

2 ripe Roma (plum) tomatoes, diced

¼ red onion, diced (about ¼ cup)

3 pickled jalapeños, diced

1 teaspoon salt

1 teaspoon ground black pepper

Juice of ½ lime

Scoop the avocado flesh into a large bowl and use a potato masher or a fork to gently smash, so there are still some chunks of avocado. Add the cilantro, tomatoes, onion, pickled jalapeños, salt, black pepper, and lime juice and mix to combine. Press a piece of plastic wrap directly against the surface of the guacamole to prevent oxidization and browning.

Refrigerate for 2 hours before serving. If there's anything left (!), store in an airtight container in the refrigerator for up to 2 days.

PICKLED ONIONS

Makes 1 cup

Total time: 30 minutes, plus overnight refrigeration

This recipe almost wasn't in the book! I used to only *buy* pickled onions, but one day, I realized it's much more affordable if you make them yourself. They cut through the richness of dishes like Chilaquiles (page 36) or any taco, and add a zing to everything from grilled chicken to guac.

1 large red onion, halved and thinly sliced (about 1 cup)

3 fresh jalapeños, thinly sliced

1 cup distilled white vinegar

½ cup fresh lime juice (about 4 limes)

1 tablespoon dried oregano

1 tablespoon granulated sugar

1 tablespoon salt

1 teaspoon ground black pepper

2 cups boiling water

Place the onion and jalapeños in a heatproof 1-quart jar. Add the vinegar, lime juice, oregano, sugar, salt, and black pepper and mix until combined. Pour the boiling water over the mixture and mix until combined. Let cool for at least 30 minutes, then close the lid and refrigerate overnight before using. Store in the refrigerator for up to 1 week.

ACKNOWLEDGMENTS

I remember when one of my very first videos, featuring my tinga recipe, went viral. I was stunned—and delighted. I couldn't believe everything that was happening at that moment. I had just started doing this for fun and didn't think it would catch on with you. I certainly didn't expect to be sharing my very own cookbook with you all just two years later! It's been quite a journey, and it's really thanks to all of you, my supporters. My life, my recipes, my vision—but I couldn't have done it without your encouragement

and the help of my amazing team. I'm so happy you all love my videos, and I hope this cookbook—packed with all my favorite recipes—will become a part of your life. I hope through these pages you'll feel why I love the kitchen. It's such an important, almost sacred place, where I can find my center, dive into my culture, express my creativity, and create delicious, enriching meals to share with my family. And you helped get me there! Thank you!

But the person who truly motivated me to cook and discover the soul-saving strength of the kitchen is my Izzy girl, my daughter. I wouldn't be where I am today without you! You are the reason this cookbook was created by pushing me into the kitchen so you could practice cutting veggies and cook alongside me. Ever since the age of two, you have always loved being in the kitchen, and your enthusiasm rubbed

off on me! You are my ray of sunshine, bringing calmness into the room with your smile and passion for cooking. I hope you pass down these recipes to your own family one day.

I also want to send a big thank-you to my husband, Brandon—a truly wonderful father and my biggest supporter. You've always believed in me, giving me the confidence to know that I can do whatever I want if I just put my mind and heart to it. You're proud of me and love my cooking (and when you don't, you're 100% honest with me about that, too!). Thanks for reminding me that I should just put it all in God's hands and everything will follow.

I want to give a huge thank-you to Justin Schwartz and his team at Simon Element for reaching out and wanting to publish a cookbook by me! I was so emotional when I first got the email from you—it was an unforgettable moment. Then, of course, a massive thanks to my managers, Rick Bhatia, Megan Frantz, and Bailey Hahn. You are the best team I could ever ask for, and I'm so glad we're doing this all together! Then I need to shout-out my literary agent, Andrea Barzvi, and my fantastic collaborator, Lauren Deen—it's been a tough but amazing journey working with you both. Thank you for helping me navigate this complicated process and allowing me to shine. Then I can't forget my recipe-testing angel, Sarah Zorn, for digging into the details to make sure my recipes were perfectly translated from my heart into clear, accurate directions you can take to your kitchens and feed to your families, like I've fed mine. And then, of course, one big reason this book is so beautiful is my amazing photographer, Ashleigh Amoroso, and her talented team, especially food stylist Ashley Holt, prop stylist Ruth Kim, food stylist assistant Katie Miller, and photo assistant Brooklyn Anderson. They translated what I saw in my mind and on my plate and turned that into the beautiful images you see here. I feel represented and grateful. *Thank you all!!!!*

INDEX

NOTE: Page references in *italics* refer to photos of recipes.

SIMON
ELEMENT

An Imprint of Simon & Schuster, LLC
1230 Avenue of the Americas
New York, NY 10020

Collaborator: Lauren Deen

Food Stylist: Ashley Holt
Prop Stylist: Ruth Kim
Food Styling Assistant: Katie Miller
Photo Assistant: Brooklyn Anderson

First Simon Element hardcover edition August 2025

SIMON ELEMENT is a trademark of Simon & Schuster, LLC

Simon & Schuster strongly believes in freedom of expression and stands against censorship in all its forms. For more information, visit BooksBelong.com.

For information about special discounts for bulk purchases, please contact Simon & Schuster Special Sales at 1-866-506-1949 or business@simonandschuster.com.

The Simon & Schuster Speakers Bureau can bring authors to your live event. For more information or to book an event, contact the Simon & Schuster Speakers Bureau at 1-866-248-3049 or visit our website at www.simonspeakers.com.

Interior design by Jen Wang

Manufactured in China

10 9 8 7 6 5 4 3 2 1

Library of Congress Cataloging-in-Publication Data has been applied for.

ISBN 978-1-6680-5130-6
ISBN 978-1-6680-5131-3 (ebook)